LESSONS LEARNED

Lessons Learned

How Good Policies Produce Better Schools

Fenton Whelan

The author is grateful for permission to reproduce the following material:
  "Stanford Achievement Test Results" from Hanushek, E., "Some Findings from an Independent Investigation of the Tennessee STAR Experiment and from Other Investigations of Class Size Effects," *Educational Evaluation and Policy Analysis 21*, 1999;
  "Relationship between student performance in science and socio-economic background for the OECD area as a whole" from OECD, *PISA 2006*, 2007.

First published 2009 in the United Kingdom by:
Fenton Whelan, 263 Croxted Road, London.

A CIP catalogue record for this book is available from the British Library.

ISBN: 978-0-9561688-0-1

Printed by the MPG Books Group in the UK

Contents

Michael Fullan is Professor Emeritus at the Ontario Institute for Studies in Education at the University of Toronto, and is recognized worldwide as an authority on education reform. Since 2003 he has been Special Advisor to the Premier and Minister of Education in Ontario, in addition to his work supporting school reforms worldwide. He has authored many books on school reform including *Leading in a Culture of Change* and *Turnaround Leadership*.

Michael Barber led the implementation of successful reforms in England's school system between 1997 and 2001 before establishing and leading the Prime Minister's Delivery Unit, a new government office created to drive improvement across the public services. He now works supporting governments and other organizations around the world to deliver tangible improvements in education. He is the author of several books including *Instruction to Deliver: Fighting to Transform Britain's Public Services* and *The Learning Game*.

Foreword

by Michael Fullan and Michael Barber

Lessons Learned is a stunningly straightforward and incisive treatment of system reform in education. Sometimes it takes an outsider to cut through the morass of complexity that system reform has accumulated over the past 50 years. Fenton Whelan has examined reforms in the Middle East, Africa, Singapore, Canada, China, Hong Kong, Finland, the United States, and a host of other OECD countries. As a member of the team that identified the characteristics of the "top performing school systems in the world" he has a strong foundation to lock into the key lessons learned.[1]

This book is about 'doing implementation,' and doing it on a large scale – the whole system. It was only slightly over a decade ago in 1997 that Tony Blair and his chief education policy architect Michael Barber launched what is arguably the first example of whole system change by basing policies and strategies on 'the change knowledge' of the day. Ontario in Canada followed suit in 2003 with its own version of systemic change strategies in action.[2] Both examples have produced promising results, but even more importantly have generated good ideas for building system reform in jurisdictions across the world.

In December 2008 education ministers and a small number of other senior leaders from eight jurisdictions convened an International Dialogue to examine what we have been learning about large-scale reform. Those present represented England, Hong Kong, Ontario, Singapore, Wales and three states from Australia (New South Wales, South Australia, and Victoria). We, along with our colleague Tony Mackay, facilitated the event.

Michael Barber made the case that it is no longer just about the right agenda, but about actually implementing it. He observed that the successful countries are moving from a series of ad hoc initiatives to a coherent, dynamic set of aligned strategies. In particular he argued that it is a matter of developing and combining three big components – the new professionalism of the entire teaching force, citizenship empowerment, and strategic leadership at all levels of the system. He said that it is about excellence and fairness, or in other words, about the high performance of all at an affordable cost.[3] He concluded that we are finally working on the right agenda which is 'professionalizing system reform' – no longer leaving it to chance or the political whims of the day.

Building especially on the work in Ontario since 2003 Michael Fullan, as the Ontario Premier's Education Adviser, emphasized that successful systems focus on a small number of ambitious goals, make capacity building linked to results the centerpiece of the strategy, and pursue these through an explicit partnership among the three levels of school and community, districts or local authorities, and the state. Doing this means mastering certain key dilemmas that have plagued the checkered history of school reform. How do you combine and reconcile: direction from the center and local choice (top-down and bottom-up forces), accountability and improvement, relentless consistency and innovativeness, raising the bar and closing the gap, and so on. He said that the current challenge is to obtain 'deep pedagogical reform', with 'systemness' (all schools), and therein to mobilize the policies, strategies, and leadership that would be required.

All of the above is what Fenton Whelan takes on with the goal of rendering it simple, but powerful in its impact. He accomplishes this with disarming clarity. He rightly notes that education has been seen as the future of civilization for over two millennia, but that few systems perform well or improve over time, despite massive increases in expenditure over the past 50 years. But some do. And this is how he gets at his seven themes – lessons to be embraced for the future. Whelan concludes that successful systems: have fewer but better teachers, get the right people to become teachers, develop effective leadership, have high standards, establish structures that empower and hold people accountable, embed professional knowledge and skills, and continuously challenge inequity. These seven themes do not just constitute a checklist. There are many subtleties, nuances, and above all sophistication in orchestrating the seven together. And Whelan does so in a clearly written engaging style never saying too much or too little, giving concrete examples in every case, and writing with flare whether talking about the world's most expensive school reform, how Finland came top in PISA, a tale of two cities, or the final chapter, the gates of paradise.

This is a time around the world in which large systems are doing serious soul searching as to why they have made virtually no progress over the past 30 years despite great quantitative effort – the United States being the prime example of failure relative to effort. The good news from *Lessons Learned* is that it does not necessarily take more money (the best systems in the world spend do not spend the most money per pupil). It takes clear thinking, tolerance, reconciling the key dilemmas we have identified above, and focusing relentlessly on a small number of core priorities – seven according to Whelan. The better news is that these themes are all amenable to policy and strategic action. The message coming through is that the problems facing system reform are fixable. It is, in other words, becoming ever clearer what to do; the challenge is to get it done.

Acknowledgements

Many hundreds of people contributed to the ideas and examples contained on these pages. I am immensely grateful to all of them for their time, for sharing their views and experiences so candidly, for taking me to their schools, for reading parts of the manuscript, and for everything from providing me with a room for the night in Kigali to an engaging debate over dinner in Muscat. To list them all would be an impossible task, however, a few made particularly significant contributions to the work.

Michael Barber and Mona Mourshed helped start me off on the journey and were a constant source of insight, debate, inspiration, and connections. This book would not have been written without them. Both Mona and Michael read parts of the manuscript and in doing so contributed much to the quality of its arguments.

Martyn Forrest taught me about getting things done in government, and provided much support while I worked on the manuscript. Professor Gopinathan and others in Singapore were a constant source of inspiration, creative thinking, clear arguments, and sound advice. Conversations with Amine Jaoui, Peter Hill, Eric Hanushek, Liz Reid, Michael Fullan, Andreas Schleicher, and Jerry Todd, though far too infrequent, always produced fresh ideas, new perspectives, and excellent discussion. Michael Fullan read the whole manuscript, contributed several key ideas, and, together with Michael Barber, graciously offered to write the foreword.

Brett Wigdortz included me in his pioneering international work while always finding time to share his own insights. He and his colleagues around the world were a constant source of intelligent criticism of different school systems and inspirational in their attempts to change those systems for the better. Hamad Al Malki and Maryam Mustafa were partners in understanding the issues from the beginning and have become great friends since. Last, but far from least, Aaron Maniam and Tara Mounce read through drafts of the manuscript, and, among many other things, provided critical comments and honest feedback when they were most needed.

Of course, any remaining errors of fact or judgement are mine alone.

Preface

The insight that education shapes the lives of individuals and societies is not a new one. Twenty three centuries have passed since Aristotle wrote that "the fate of empires rests on the education of youth." Fourteen centuries ago the Imperial Examination System was established in China, affirming the importance of education to the fate of individuals and the Empire in what was the first national standards-based education reform. Two hundred years ago, as the United States was founded, Thomas Jefferson counselled that "if a nation expects to be ignorant and free, in a state of civilization, it expects what never was and never will be."

Over the past century, changes in the global economy and the spread of democracy have raised the value and importance of education even further. Economic growth depends increasingly on ever more skilled and innovative workforces, democratic politics demands citizens who can make and evaluate complex decisions about how society should function, while tackling the multidimensional problems of climate change and cultural clash requires each us to make informed choices about how we live our daily lives. Improving education is high up on the political agenda of almost every country in the world, and commands a global budget from governments in excess of three trillion dollars each year.

Yet, despite great increases in spending and numerous reforms, few school systems perform well. In most, large numbers of students, particularly those from poorer backgrounds, fail to acquire even the most basic skills, despite the fact that some school systems prove that every child can be taught to read, write, and do mathematics to a good level. In many, significant numbers of schools are failing or dysfunctional, even though some countries have long proved that a school system does not have to have bad schools. While most professions and industries have changed beyond recognition over the past few decades, much of what happens in schools has stayed almost exactly the same.

This book began in the Middle East as part of a series of projects to find ways to improve the region's schools. The work sought inspiration from school systems in countries with strong records of educational achievement. The approach was to scour the world, looking at what had worked and how it might be applied in the Middle East. The process and questions were rarely theoretical, but rather intensely practical and focused: what did you do, how did you do it, what impact did it have, and what would you do differently if you had to do it again?

Over time, that journey took on new purposes, but the questions remained the same. So far, it has taken me from the cities of China to the plains of Siberia, to the grasslands of Africa, and to the streets of New York. It has captured lessons about school reform from more than 40 countries on every continent. The lessons were sometimes interesting for their differences, but more often they were striking for their similarities. The same patterns emerged over and over again, the same solutions worked, and the same mistakes were made.

This book is an attempt to draw those lessons together. It centres on questions of how to make the system work. Understanding what makes a good mathematics lesson or, more broadly, how to improve teaching and learning in individual classrooms, is extremely important to improving education. But even more important is finding ways to deliver that good teaching and learning across an entire system; one which may contain hundreds of thousands of teachers working in tens of thousands of schools. How do you get every mathematics lesson to be a good mathematics lesson? How do you get every school to be a good school?

Perhaps the most exciting thing about education at the beginning of the 21ˢᵗ century, two and a half millennia after the establishment of the world's first compulsory school systems, is that answers to those questions are beginning to emerge. New international assessments, improved data, and the ceaseless work of researchers and policymakers have produced a wealth of knowledge about what works and why. Sometimes that understanding is inaccessible to those who influence and make decisions about education policy – hidden in academic journals or obscured by a fog of political controversy and popular opinion – but it is emerging nonetheless. Out of that understanding, four things stand out.

The first thing we know is that just spending more money and employing more teachers does not help much. Luxembourg, Norway, and Iceland spend more on their schools than almost any other government in the world, yet they all perform below the developed-country average. South Korea, Finland, and New Zealand spend less than most other developed countries, yet they achieve some of the highest performance in the world. Developed countries with the smallest class sizes are often among the lowest performing, while those with the largest class sizes are sometimes among the best. They show that achieving good performance is not about how much money is spent or how many teachers are employed, but how well that money is spent and how well those teachers teach.

The second thing we know is that the key to transforming learning in schools is changing what happens inside classrooms. A child who starts school at age four and graduates at age 18 will spend roughly one million minutes at school. What they learn at school is essentially the sum of what they learn during each of those one million minutes. The research shows that how much they learn depends mainly on the teachers they are taught by and the schools which they attend. Students with the best teachers in the best schools learn at least three times more each year than students with the worst teachers in the worst schools. Unless reforms change and improve the detail of what happens inside schools and classrooms, they are unlikely to change outcomes.

The third thing we know is that most school systems have struggled to improve, but a few prove that substantial and sustained improvement over time is possible. In the United States, there has been almost no measurable improvement in the skills of students leaving school for the past four decades. One influential study showed that across a range of developed-world school systems, few had improved over a 25-year period and several had got worse. Yet some school systems have improved. Singapore moved from low levels of education at its independence in 1965 to some of the highest performance in the world. Several school districts, states, and provinces in the United States and Canada have achieved big improvements in outcomes over the past decade. Finland tops the world in educational achievement despite spending less on its schools than its neighbours. Together, those systems show that high performance and continuous improvement are possible.

The fourth thing we know is how to do it. There are many things which a school system and the people who work in it need to get right in order to make sure that every child is able to learn. They need to ensure that school buildings are warm and welcoming, that school buses depart and arrive on time, that school meals are nutritious, that parents and community organizations are involved in schools, and that children are safe from harm during their time at school. However, when it comes to ensuring that children leave school with the values, skills, and knowledge they need to succeed, seven themes lie at the core of building a successful school system. They are:

- having *fewer but better teachers*;
- getting the *right people* to become teachers;

- ensuring that every school has *effective leadership*;
- setting high *standards* and measuring whether they are achieved;
- creating *structures* which empower people, hold them accountable, and encourage collaboration;
- investing in building teachers' *professional knowledge and skills*; and
- continuously *challenging inequity* in educational performance.

The first chapter of this book sets out the argument that massive improvement in schools is possible. The following seven chapters explore each of the themes above in turn. The final chapter looks at the broader challenge of delivering a coherent and successful school reform. Together, they argue that the right policies combined with excellent delivery can make every school a great school, help every teacher to become an effective teacher, and ensure that all children receive the one million minutes of excellent schooling they deserve.

1.

One million minutes
and the fate of empires

(Why education matters and how to improve it)

Twenty three centuries ago, Aristotle wrote that "the fate of empires rests of the education of youth." In the modern world, more than ever before, education determines the fate of individuals and societies: how much people will earn, how happy they will be, how fast economies will grow, and how many people will get left behind. Governments spend large and increasing amounts of money on education and most engage in continuous and wide-ranging reforms. Yet few of those reforms have had the impact their designers hoped for and, in many school systems, there has been little improvement in student outcomes for decades. In most countries, large numbers of students fail to reach even the most basic levels of proficiency. However, a small number of school systems do deliver consistently good schooling, do ensure that every child reaches a good standard of achievement, and do improve over time. More importantly, we know a lot about how they do it.

Why education matters

Education has long been known to benefit individuals and societies. Twenty five centuries ago, the city of Sparta proved that a strong school system could be the foundation for a successful and enduring state. More than two millennia have passed since governments in Greece and Israel recognized the value of universal education by establishing the first compulsory school systems. In the 20th century, several East Asian countries showed that a good school system could be one of the main drivers of rapid economic and social development. All of the evidence suggests that in the 21st century, education will be more important than ever before.

Modern economies require increasingly better educated workforces to sustain growth and prosperity. The number of jobs which demand a high level of skills is rising rapidly, while the number of low-skill jobs is falling as routine work is increasingly automated or outsourced to the countries with the lowest wages.[1] At the same time, economic development is increasingly driven by innovation and the creation of new technologies, both of which demand a highly educated workforce. One report counsels that "the most effective modern economies will be those that produce the most information and knowledge."[2] Across the world as a whole, the benefits from and returns to education are rising over time,[3] and countries with higher levels of education are developing faster, producing more knowledge, and innovating more than countries with lower levels of education.[4]

The economic and financial returns to education are even more pronounced for individuals. Workers with higher levels of education earn more and are less likely to be unemployed than others, often by a considerable margin.[5] In the United States, for instance, holders of professional degrees earn four times more than people without a high-school certificate.[6] Even more important than the amount of education people complete is how much they learn along the way.[7] For instance, workers with the lowest literacy scores are up to twenty times more likely to be unemployed than those with the highest literacy scores.[8] Scores in numeracy and literacy tests as early as age seven have been found to be strong predictors of a person's earnings when they are in their mid-30s, even after controlling for the effect of their socioeconomic background. In fact, these tests scores from primary school are better predictors of how much a person will earn in their 30s than whether they have a university degree.[9]

Good education systems produce a range of non-financial benefits as well. Better educated people are happier and more content with their lives, even after accounting for the fact that they have higher incomes.[10] They are also more likely to have good diets, healthy lifestyles, fewer serious illnesses, and a lower chance of involvement in criminal activity. These effects can be extremely large: in some African countries, for instance, secondary school graduates are five times less likely to contract HIV than people who have not been to school,[11] while in the United States, black men who complete twelve years of schooling are six times less likely to spend time in prison than those who complete only nine.[12] Higher levels of education across societies as a whole have been linked to the spread of democracy, more informed voting patterns in elections, the reduction of violence, and the prevention of war.[13] The scale of all of these effects is increasing over time so that more than ever before, the fate of individuals and societies – how happy they will be, how much they will earn, how fast their economies will grow, and how many people will be left behind – all depend on how well nations educate their youth.

Given the scale and importance of that challenge, it is unsurprising that countries spend large and increasing amounts of money on education. Total public spending on education currently exceeds three trillion dollars each year and most developed countries have more than doubled their education spending over the past four decades.[14] At the same time, there has been a sustained effort to try to improve the effectiveness with which that money is spent. Until the events of September 2001 changed the course of his presidency, George Bush described education reform as "the cornerstone of [his] administration."[15] When Tony Blair told the press that his top three priorities in government would be "education, education, and education," then Prime Minister John Major responded that his priorities were the same "but not necessarily in that order." Improving education tops the political agenda in almost every community in the world, from African townships to the streets of Manhattan.

Yet despite increased spending and repeated attempts to reform, few school systems come close to delivering on the challenge of providing consistently high-quality education for every child. In most, a significant number of children fail to acquire even basic skills. More importantly, few school systems appear to be improving over time.

Few school systems perform well or improve over time

One of the longest records of student performance over time comes from the American state of Iowa. Every year since 1935, the creators of a standardized test known as the Iowa Test of Basic Skills have tested a representative sample of students in Iowa's schools in order to determine the average level of academic achievement in the State. Importantly, the testing and sampling are done in a way that makes it possible to compare test scores in one year to test scores in another. The results give us a uniquely reliable picture of how educational outcomes have changed over a period of more than 70 years.

Between 1935 and 1966, the test results showed that there was constant improvement at all grade levels.[16] In 1966, students graduating from Iowan schools had higher levels of literacy and numeracy than every cohort that had preceded them. It was around the time that this best-educated generation of Iowans in history entered adulthood that the Iowa caucuses became the first major event in the presidential electoral season, giving Iowans a disproportionately large influence over who becomes president of the United States. Unfortunately, 1966 was the peak year. The test scores entered a slow decline that lasted through to the end of the 1970s. There was some improvement during the 1980s, followed by another decline during the 1990s, and then a slight rise after the millennium.[17] Overall, test scores in Iowa today are still much higher than they were in 1935, but about the same as they were in the mid 1960s.

The same story of constant levels of achievement in schools over the past four decades appears to be true for the United States as a whole. The earliest representative national record of educational performance for the United States comes from a testing program run by the Department of Education called the National Assessment of Educational Progress (NAEP).[18] NAEP was established by Congress in 1969, and has been testing American school students in subjects including mathematics, science, reading, and writing since the early 1970s. The test program includes two separate assessment schemes: one which is kept constant from year to year so that it produces a reliable picture of trends in academic achievement over time, and another which is updated periodically so that it provides current data which is consistent with changing emphases in curriculum and standards. Tests are conducted once every two years and, since 1992, have included large enough samples of students to produce accurate scores for individual states.

The NAEP scores show that the average level of literacy and numeracy among Americans leaving school today is almost exactly the same as it was when the tests started. In both reading and mathematics, there is no difference between the scores of 17-year olds today and the scores of the 17-year olds who took the first tests in the 1970s, though there have been recent gains at the lower grades.[19] This is despite a massive increase in spending and resources. Between 1971 and 2004, the United States more than doubled its spending on every student in the school system.[20] It also employed more teachers. By 2004, there were almost one and half times as many teachers, relative to the number of students, as there had been in 1971, and class sizes were the smallest in American history.[21] Yet after decades of increasing spending and relentless reform, the achievement levels of students leaving school were still almost exactly the same.

Other school systems faced similar problems with improvement. In England, an influential study found that there was no improvement in average levels of literacy and numeracy in schools between

1948 and 1996 and, more strikingly, that there had been little change to the pattern of a significant number of students failing to acquire basic literacy and numeracy skills since "at least the generation which entered school around 1925."[22] The following year, Tony Blair became Prime Minister, declaring that "no one ever believes that anything happens in education and we will prove them wrong."[23] Reforms implemented during the late 1990s did produce a real improvement in standards of numeracy and literacy.[24] However, progress slowed after the first few years and in some areas the results reached a plateau. International tests suggested that performance in reading in 2006 was slightly lower than it had been in 2001, though mathematics and science scores had continued to rise.[25]

This same picture of constant levels of achievement despite relentless spending and reform is repeated in almost every developed country for which there is reliable long-term data.[26] In 2003, a seminal study compared changes in the performance of schools in eleven developed countries between 1970 and 1995. In all of the countries, education spending had risen dramatically, and in all but three of the countries, that rise in education spending had outpaced the overall growth of the economy. Yet none of the countries was able to create a substantial improvement in the performance of its school system, and in most, performance declined. The highest increases in education spending were in Australia, New Zealand, and France, all of which more than tripled their spending on education per student over the 25-year period. In all three, mathematics and science scores either stayed the same or got worse.[27]

One explanation for that lack of improvement would be that schools have already become as effective as they can be. However, there is plenty of evidence that most schools and most school systems could be performing much better. For instance, the following graph shows the percentage of children in different countries who fail to acquire basic reading skills by the age of 10. Literacy at age 10 is one of the best measures of the health of a school system, partly because reading is an important skill in and of itself, but also because it is one of the most important determinants of success in the rest of schooling and life after graduation. Children who cannot read well by age 10 will struggle to access the rest of the curriculum and will find it increasingly difficult to make good progress in other subjects. As they begin to fail across a range of subjects, that failure creates additional problems with behaviour, attention in class, and interest in school work. They quickly fall further and further behind to the point at which that failure is essentially irreversible. A wealth of evidence suggests that the effects of not acquiring basic literacy by that age on the rest of an individual's life are severe and difficult to address.[28]

Reading ability at age ten is also a good measure of the performance of a school system because there is no good reason why any child in a wealthy country, except for a very small minority of children in extremely difficult circumstances, should not be able to read well by age 10. Every developed country in the world possesses the knowledge, curricula, teachers, and resources to ensure that every child is able to read, and has done for some time. If a significant proportion of children cannot read, that represents a clear failure of the system.

A number of school systems, among them Hong Kong, the Netherlands, the Canadian province of Alberta, Flemish Belgium, and Lithuania, prove that it is possible to ensure that every child can read well by age 10. However, in most school systems a significant number of children get left behind. In many developed countries up to 10% of students fail to acquire basic reading skills by age 10, and even this threshold represents a lower level of literacy than what would be required to fully access most secondary curricula. In a few wealthy countries in the Middle East, more than half of all students fail to acquire basic literacy skills.

Figure 1: Percentage of children aged 10 with very low reading skills in selected countries and school systems

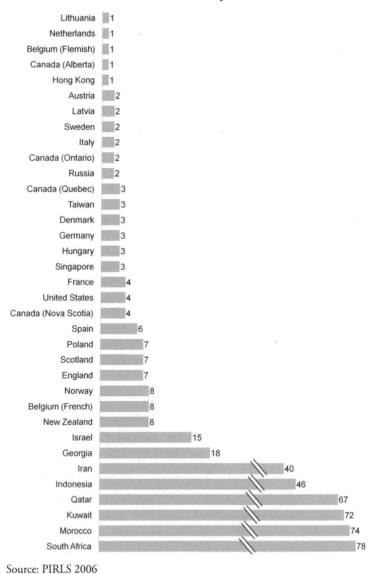

Source: PIRLS 2006

Notably, the countries which have been most successful in ensuring that every child learns how to read include medium-income countries such as Russia and Lithuania, while those which have been least successful include two of the three richest countries in the world: Norway and Qatar. Among developed countries, there is almost no relationship between GDP per capita and educational performance. There is also no discernible relationship between the number of immigrants or the diversity of a country's population and its educational performance. For instance, Australia, New Zealand, and Canada, where more than 20% of students have parents who are first-generation immigrants, all outperform Japan where 99.6% of the school population is native Japanese. There are no particular cultural patterns either: there are wide variations in performance between different Canadian provinces, the five Scandinavian countries, and different countries in East Asia; while the international top-performers include Singapore, South Korea, Finland, Canada, and Cuba, five countries with very different histories, cultures, and traditions. Overall, among developed countries, there are almost no detectable cultural, demographic, or economic factors which explain why some school systems perform better than others. Rather, the differences seem to be driven by characteristics of the school systems themselves.

In the face of criticism that schools are not improving or that failure persists unchallenged, many commentators have argued that massive improvement in educational outcomes is impossible. Some argue that educational performance is determined mainly by a combination of immutable variables, including the intrinsic abilities of the students, the culture in which they grow up, and the families into which they are born. The argument is made, both implicitly and explicitly, that whether children succeed at school is largely the result of who they are, who their parents are, and where they grow up. Faced with these intrinsic factors, schooling and school policy can have little impact on overall outcomes (if true, this would be a good reason to stop increasing education spending). This argument was popularised in part by a set of influential (though flawed) studies conducted during the 1960s, most notably the Coleman Report,[29] which purported to demonstrate that the quality of schooling had no measurable effect on educational achievement. Others argue that schools do matter and have been improving, but that every improvement in school quality is matched by an equal and opposite deterioration in social conditions which makes students progressively harder to teach or less willing to learn. This argument dates back at least to Hesiod in the 8th century BCE, who wrote: "I see no hope for the future of our people if they are dependent on frivolous youth of today, for certainly all youth are reckless beyond words." Because the characteristics of students entering the school system are always declining, outcomes remain constant, even though the effectiveness of the school system is actually improving.

However, there are good reasons to believe that substantial improvement in education outcomes is possible: that the problems of inequity, school failure, poor teaching, and low levels of achievement can be addressed and solved. One reason for believing that massive improvement is possible is that there has been little change in schools during a period in which every other sector of the economy has been transformed. Another is the fact that some schools perform much better than others, which suggests that those others could do better. However, the most compelling reason for believing that substantial improvement is possible, is the fact that there are good examples of how to do it.

Some school systems demonstrate that substantial improvement over time is possible

When Singapore gained its independence in 1965 almost half of its population was illiterate.[30] Two thirds of students dropped out of school before the end of tenth grade, and only one student in ten gained three or more O-level passes.[31] Schools were organized by ethnicity, exacerbating racial tensions and reinforcing linguistic and cultural barriers between communities. Simultaneously, Singapore's government faced the challenges of low overall levels of development, poor infrastructure, high unemployment, and political and ethnic tensions.

During the three decades that followed, the government relentlessly reformed and improved the school system. It massively expanded secondary enrolment and doubled the size of the teaching profession. It kept class sizes large rather than compromising on the quality of new teachers or lowering teacher salaries. It set high expectations for student achievement and linked its examinations to the British A-level and O-level system to ensure that they received wide recognition and to prevent slippage in standards. It invested heavily in teacher training and constantly worked to improve the leadership and management of the system.

By 1995, 30 years after independence, Singapore had one of the top-performing school systems in the world. In international tests of science and mathematics, Singaporean eighth graders ranked first in the world.[32] However, there was still scope for improvement. Singaporean fourth graders scored top in the world in mathematics, however they lagged behind other countries in science. Reading skills in English were still a problem; in 2001, international tests showed that Singaporean 10-year olds had lower levels of literacy that their peers in most English-speaking countries.[33] Employers were critical of the school system's ability to nurture creativity and innovation. No Singaporean has ever been awarded a Nobel Prize; in the words of one research leader: "We produce good imitators and efficient managers, but not creative entrepreneurs." Thirty years of relentless reform had produced a good school system, but not a great one.

So the reform continued. Singapore introduced creative thinking throughout the curriculum. It continued to recruit its teachers only from the top third of high-school graduates, and rigorously screened applicants to ensure that it got the right people into the teaching profession. It raised starting salaries for teachers so that they were in-line with starting salaries for other professions – lawyers, accountants, civil servants, and engineers. It adapted leadership programs from the private sector to create a six-month full-time leadership program for aspiring school principals. It introduced a new performance management scheme for teachers adapted from a leading multinational company with regular developmental evaluation, performance-based bonuses, and an entitlement of 100 hours of in-service training for every teacher every year. It created a culture of high performance and commitment to success in its schools, with teachers working together to help students to achieve. Many teachers in Singaporean schools give out their cell phone numbers to students, and expect them to call at any time if they have problems with homework or need help in the run up to exams.

By 2005, 40 years after independence, Singaporean students scored top in the world in science and mathematics at both grade 4 and grade 8.[34] More strikingly, between 2001 and 2005,[35] Singapore increased the average reading scores of ten-year olds in English on international tests by an additional 30 points, equivalent to almost a year of schooling. The result is some of the highest academic performance in the world. By age 10, students in Singapore now have higher reading scores in English than students in any English-speaking country, including Canada, the United States, England, Scotland, and New Zealand. Many of these students come from homes where English is not the first language and all of them have to learn their mother-tongue language (Chinese, Malay, or Tamil) in addition to English. Raffles Junior College, the top-performing high school in Singapore, sends more students to Ivy League universities in the United States than any other school in the world. In 40 years, Sin-

gapore created a school system which produces the highest performance in the world on almost every measure of academic achievement,
and which continues to improve. It still spends less on each student
in its schools than any other developed country.[36]

Some schools get excellent results in tough areas

The Knowledge Is Power Program (KIPP) is a chain of 66 charter
schools serving students in high-poverty areas across the United
States.[37] KIPP schools enrol some of the most disadvantaged students
in the United States. On average, four out of five come from low-
income families, and 19 out of 20 are from ethnic minorities. These
are children who would normally have less than a 50-50 chance of

Figure 2: Change in reading scores of children aged 10 in selected countries between 2001 and 2005/6

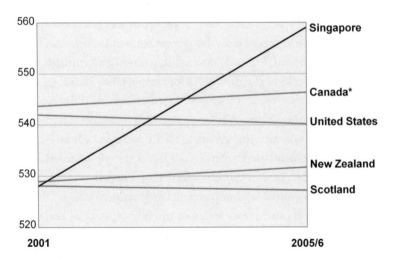

* For Canada scores include Ontario and Quebec only
Source: *PIRLS 2001* and *PIRLS 2006*

graduating from high school, and a one in five chance of going to college.

KIPP was started in 1994 by two teachers – Mike Feinberg and Dave Levin. Fresh out of college, they had started teaching at a school in Houston in 1992 as members of the Teach For America program. During their first term, the other teachers in the school placed bets on whether they would last through to Thanksgiving.[38] By their second year, Levin and Feinberg had discovered a lot about what it took to get kids from tough backgrounds to learn. But they had also discovered that the problem of educational underachievement in high-poverty areas was, at least in part, caused by systemic failings and inefficiencies in the schools themselves. So they decided to develop a school model that worked, setting up a new charter school in Houston centred around high aspirations, strong leadership, quality teaching, and longer school hours. The called the school the KIPP Academy.

The model they developed remained essentially unchanged as the network of schools expanded. Students in KIPP schools spend 60% more time at school than the average student in America. They are in school from 0730 to 1700 each day, alternate Saturdays, and for six extra weeks in the summer. More importantly, KIPP ensures that the time they spend in school is used effectively. Principals in KIPP schools are the lynchpin for establishing a culture of high performance and constant improvement. KIPP looks for school leaders who are "student-focused, relentless achievers, people-oriented, self-aware, adaptable, critical thinkers and decision makers, strong communicators, organized, and inspirational instructional leaders."[39] The selection process includes a series of interviews, tests of teaching practice, and a two-day assessment centre. Once selected, principals embark on a one-year training program which includes time spent being coached by KIPP principals in their schools and course material delivered jointly by the Graduate School of Business and the

School of Education at Stanford.

Principals carefully select the right people to teach in the schools, often paying higher salaries to help attract the best. In the schools, they create a culture of high expectations and high performance, with a strong commitment to doing what it takes to make every student succeed. Students, parents, and teachers sign contracts committing themselves to achieving academic excellence. When asked, every student in a KIPP school can tell you the year when they will start College. They have precise learning objectives for every week, written on the walls of classrooms starting with the phrase "by the end of this week I will be able to ... ." Students wear t-shirts with the guiding principles of the KIPP code – "Work Hard. Be Nice" – across the back. Every teacher writes their cell phone number on the wall of their classroom, and pledges to answer calls from students who need help with work at any time. A sign over the entrance to one KIPP school reads, "Welcome to the home of the hardest working kids in America."

So far, four out of every five students from KIPP schools have gone on to college. In their first year of middle school, students at some KIPP schools make three times more progress than average students, and five times more progress than students in schools with comparable enrolment. That means that they learn every eight weeks what students in comparable schools learn in a whole year. The first class of students at the Key Academy, a KIPP school in Washington D.C., entered at the 34th percentile in mathematics and graduated four years later at the 92nd percentile.[40] Collectively, KIPP schools have some of the highest performance in the United States.[41]

Neither KIPP nor Singapore has the perfect model for managing a school system. Nor are they the only examples of school systems which have delivered consistently high levels of performance and improvement. Cuba, Finland, South Korea, and Hong Kong all have strong performance records, as do several Canadian and Chinese provinces. All of these models succeed in part because of factors which might be absent in other school systems. Singapore's schools draw on a strong cultural and political commitment to education. KIPP attracts a quality of teachers and principals which would be difficult to find for a much larger number of schools. Cuba spends a greater proportion of its national income on education than would be feasible in most other countries, and teaching is attractive as a career choice in part because of a lack of opportunities elsewhere in the economy. Yet these school systems are important, because they represent relatively rare instances of school systems which consistently produce high performance and strong improvement, and because the reasons why they succeed – among them, selecting the right people to become teachers, good professional development, effective school leadership, and a culture of high expectations and commitment to doing what it takes to achieve them – are fundamentally the same. Their record of improvement, combined with the fact that it seems to be a consistent set of policies, rather than unique individual circumstances, which lead to high performance, suggests that most schools could be much better, and that most of the secrets for achieving that are already known.

The main challenge for any school system is to provide every child with one million minutes of quality instruction

A child who starts school at age four and graduates at age 18 will spend roughly one million minutes at school. What they learn during their time at school is essentially the sum of what they learn during each of those one million minutes. The quality of those classroom experiences is what drives learning, and it is differences in the quality of those classroom experiences which must drive differences in how much students learn at school. This is probably the most frequently overlooked truism about the performance of schools: that learning happens in classrooms, and that differences in how much students learn at school must ultimately be the result of differences in what happens in classrooms. By implication, effective schools and school systems are only effective to the extent that they create the conditions under which effective classroom teaching occurs.

What the research on performance in schools consistently shows is that differences in the quality of learning between classrooms are extremely large, and that those differences explain much of the overall variation in student outcomes. A series of seminal studies conducted in the United States during the mid-1990s found that for any five teachers, students taught by the most effective teacher would make three times as much progress over the course of a year as students taught by the least effective teacher.[42] Over a period of several years, these effects were cumulative, with students taught by good teachers moving further and further ahead, while students taught by less effective teachers fell further and further behind. Moreover, teacher quality had residual effects on student learning in later years as well. A student taught by a good teacher in their first year at school would make more progress in their second year than a student who had been taught by a less effective teacher in their first year, even if they were now in the same class with the same teacher. In combination, these effects were substantial: an average student at the 50th percentile who was assigned three effective teachers in a row would reach the 90th percentile after three years, while an average student assigned three ineffective teachers in a row would fall to the 37th percentile.

A range of studies conducted in other parts of the world have drawn similar conclusions. One study conducted in Australia found that teacher quality impacted student outcomes more than any other variable throughout both primary and secondary schooling. In English, teacher quality was found to be responsible for 40% of the variation in student performance, while in Mathematics, it was responsible for more than 50% of the variation in student performance.[43] For the Australian students, "when all other sources of variation are taken into account, including gender, social backgrounds of students, and differences between schools, the largest differences in student achievement are between classes. By far the most important source of variation in student achievement is teacher quality."[44]

None of this is surprising. Tales of exceptional teachers fostering exceptional learning are as much part of the folklore of every school as they are part of the experiences of every school child. Increasing amounts of data simply allow us to confirm empirically that some teachers are massively more effective than others. One teacher working in a KIPP school in Washington D.C. took a class of students from the 16th percentile in mathematics to the 77th percentile, the greatest amount of progress ever achieved by a class of students in a KIPP school in a single year.[45] At the other end of the spectrum, the Boston school district in the United States found that high-school students placed with the least effective math teachers in the city actually regressed over the course of the year; their mathematics scores got worse. Together, the research shows that more than anything else, how much a student learns at school is determined by how many good teachers they get, and how many bad teachers they get. In the words of one superintendent: "We are truly beholden to teachers because teachers determine, in many instances, who will live in poverty and who will live with some measure of prosperity. Teachers frequently determine who gets to read, write, compute, and go on to post-secondary. Teachers say things and do things that stick with you for your whole life."[46]

The implication is that the main task of any school system is to ensure that every child is taught by a series of great teachers; that their one million minutes of classroom experience are of the highest possible quality. Clearly lots of different things impact how much a child learns at school, and how relevant what they have learned is to what they actually need to know, understand, or be able to do once they have left school. School systems need to ensure that their curricula are relevant and contain enough flexibility to accommodate different learners and different social and economic needs. They need to ensure that school buildings are in good condition, that bills are paid on time, that health and safety regulations are adhered to, and that school buses depart on time. All these things are important, and ultimately impact academic performance.

However, none is nearly as important as the quality of teaching. For instance, research studies which try to measure whether one curriculum is better than another consistently find that the variation between different teachers using the same curriculum or textbook is so large as to render any experimental comparison of the curricula themselves meaningless: "50 years of research on classroom teaching indicates that it is how teachers implement and adapt particular methods and materials that sits at the core of instructional effectiveness, not the curricula themselves."[47]

Moreover, none of the other challenges that a school system faces are as difficult to achieve as improving and sustaining the quality of classroom teaching. Many school systems employ tens of thousands of teachers, working simultaneously in tens of thousands of classrooms, spread out over vast areas. India alone has more than one million schools. In Russia and Canada, many schools are located in areas which are inaccessible by road for parts of the year. In all school systems, teachers work, for the most part, alone and without direct oversight; in the language of the business world, they are a distributed field force. Ensuring that every child gets one million minutes of quality teaching, when the people who deliver that teaching are so highly dispersed, is not easy.

The challenge is complicated by the fact that the outcomes which we expect teachers to deliver – numeracy and literacy, character development, creativity, values, and sensitivity, to name a few – are various, complex, and in many cases, difficult to measure, as are the conditions under which teachers are expected to deliver them. All of these factors combine to make the challenge of raising the quality of classroom teaching a difficult one: changing the actions of a group of people you cannot see, doing a set of things you cannot easily measure, and under circumstances which require each of them to adopt a different approach in order to achieve them.

This also explains much of the lack of improvement. Over the past four decades, governments have spent more money on schools, hired more teachers, reformed curricula, changed structures, introduced technology, and made numerous other changes to their school systems. However, in most cases, relatively little has changed inside the classroom. As one education reformer in England puts it: "From 1988 to 1998 we experienced 10 years of unrelenting education reform, 10 years in which everything we could see in the education universe was reformed, reviewed, reorganised. [England reformed ...] the funding of schools, the governance of schools, curriculum standards, assessment and testing, the training of teachers, the professional development of teachers, the inspection of quality, the role of local government, the role of national government, the range and nature of national agencies, the relationship of schools to parents and communities, school admissions, and so on. Between 1988 and 1998, all these things were changed, changed utterly, sometimes twice or three times. And then I'd go into a primary school classroom in 1998 and I'd think to myself – this is very like 1988."[48] Unless reforms change what teachers do in classrooms, they are unlikely to change student outcomes.

No set of schools has cracked the secret of delivering high-quality education across the system. Even the best schools and school systems have their imperfections. Nonetheless, there is a growing body of evidence about how to improve and sustain a higher quality of classroom instruction. There is a set of schools and school systems which collectively demonstrate what can be done to improve performance. There are lessons from the business sector which can be applied in education. And there are growing amounts of quantitative evidence from national and international assessments which can be used to identify the approaches which work and those which do not. Out of that evidence, seven lessons emerge for improving performance in school systems:

- Have fewer but better teachers
- Get the right people to become teachers
- Ensure that every school has effective leadership
- Set high standards and measure whether they are achieved
- Create structures which empower people, hold them accountable, and encourage collaboration
- Invest in building teachers' professional knowledge and skills
- Continuously challenge inequity in educational performance

The coming chapters explore each of those themes in more detail.

2.

The world's most expensive school reform

(Why more teachers means less learning)

Reducing class sizes is one of the most popular, widely implemented, and extensively-funded reforms aimed at improving learning in schools. Unfortunately, it does little to improve student outcomes. In experimental settings, students in small classes make almost the same amount of progress as students in large classes. However, reducing class sizes across an entire school system has serious implications for teacher quality. School systems which have smaller classes need more teachers, which in turn means that they can be less selective about who becomes a teacher, pay lower salaries, and invest less in developing and supporting each teacher. That is important because the evidence consistently shows that what matters is not whether there are 25 or 15 students in a classroom, but whether there is a good teacher in the classroom. As a result, reducing class sizes actually leads to lower student outcomes. This effect is substantial, and among developed countries, explains more of the variation in performance between school systems than any other policy choice.

Reducing class sizes rarely leads to improvement in student outcomes

Academic achievement in schools in the State of California has long been among the lowest in the United States. Since the federal government started collecting data on the educational performance of individual states in 1992, average mathematics and reading scores have always placed California among the bottom five states in the

Union. By the eighth grade, the difference between the reading scores of students in Massachusetts and students in California is equivalent to two and a half years of schooling. The difference between their mathematics scores is equivalent to almost three years of schooling. The state's poor record of educational performance is partly explained by its unique demographics: California's population has the highest proportion of recent immigrants in the United States.[1] However, even when allowances are made for the range of challenges faced by California's schools, their performance is still poor compared to the rest of the United States.[2]

In response to that poor record of performance, California's policymakers embarked on what was, at the time, the most expensive education reform in history. In the summer of 1996, incentives were introduced to encourage schools to reduce class sizes in kindergarten and the first three grades (K-3) to a maximum of 20 students in each class. At the time, California's classes, with an average of 29 students, were the largest in the United States. The stated aim of the initiative was to "increase student achievement, particularly in reading and mathematics."[3] Within three years, the reduction in class size had largely been achieved. More than 98% of Californian students in the targeted grades were in classes of 20 students or less.

During the first ten years of implementation, the initiative cost 15 billion dollars, or 900 dollars for each student each year. Its record as the most expensive school reform in history was only beaten when the State of Florida introduced its own class size reduction program six years later.

The problem was that the initiative did not have much impact on how much Californian students learned at school. Before the start of the class size reduction program, California ranked 49th among the 50 states in fourth grade reading. Eleven years later in 2007, it ranked 48th.[4] California's one place rise in the rankings was caused principally by the fact that reading scores in Louisiana, which had been marginally ahead of California in 2005, fell slightly in the wake of Hurricane Katrina, allowing California to edge into the third from last spot. In mathematics, California's rank among the 50 states rose from 48th place to 47th place. Though the absolute level of achievement in California's schools did improve slightly over the ten year period, the improvement was less than the average for the United States as a whole, and less than the improvement in those states which did not make large reductions in class sizes.

Long-term evaluations found that the class size reduction had no effect on academic achievement in Californian schools. To its credit, California had established an independent academic panel to evaluate the impact of the initiative. During the first couple of years, some studies found a small but significant increase in performance as a result of the reduced class sizes; for instance, students in the smaller classes performed a few points higher on reading tests than similar students in larger classes. However, later studies showed that after correcting for student background (students from more wealthy backgrounds were more likely to be in smaller classes during those first two years) the students who benefited from reduced class sizes performed no better than those who did not.[5] The State's own official evaluation of the initiative concluded that while there had been some improvement in educational performance in California over the period as a whole, the "attribution of gains in scores to class size reduction is not warranted."[6]

California has not been alone in reducing class sizes. In fact, almost every school system in the developed world has reduced its student-to-teacher ratio over the past two decades. Since 1996, 29 out of 30 countries in the OECD and 48 out of 50 American states have reduced their student-to-teacher ratios, employing more teachers for every student in their schools.[7] Thirty-two American states currently have class size reduction initiatives in place. Surveys of parents and teachers find that it is one of the most popular ideas for improving schools; in the words of one major journal: "Of all the ideas for improving education, few are as simple and attractive as reducing the number of pupils per teacher."[8] The OECD describes class size reduction as "probably the most widely supported and extensively funded policy aimed at improving schools."[9]

Yet, across a wide range of school systems which have reduced class sizes, there is little evidence that there has been any improvement in educational outcomes as a result. Australia, the United Kingdom, and France all made large reductions in class sizes over the past few decades, without seeing any consequent improvement in overall student performance. In the United States, the average class size fell from 27 to 21 between 1971 and 2001, yet the test scores of students leaving school remained exactly the same. Moreover, the states which reduced their class sizes the most were among the slowest to improve. The three states with the largest reductions in their student-to-teacher ratios between 1995 and 2005 were Alaska, North Dakota, and Rhode Island.[10] All of them registered a decline in performance relative to the rest of the United States over that same period.[11] Across a wide range of developed counties and school systems, class size reduction has been implemented, but almost invariably without any discernible effect on student performance.

Why class size doesn't matter (much)

In theory, there are two main reasons why smaller classes might increase student achievement. First, smaller class sizes might be easier for teachers to control, freeing up more time for focused teaching and learning. Second, smaller classes might allow teachers to devote more time to each student, thereby allowing them to provide more individualized instruction. In general, it is the combination of these effects which has been used to justify class size reduction policies.

The best way to determine how big those effects are would be to run an experiment in which students were randomly assigned to classes of different sizes with all other variables held constant. The performance of the students could be measured, and inferences drawn about the effects of class size as a result. Unfortunately, the number of reliable experimental studies of this type is very small. There has only been one major experimental study into the effect of class size on student achievement, conducted in the 1980s, in addition to a few smaller studies. All of these studies have significant flaws, and none of them gives us a robust understanding of the relationships between class size, teaching, and student achievement. Crucially, none of them have looked at the effect of class size on learning beyond the first few grades of schooling.

The lack of reliable evidence on the effects of class size on student achievement is itself indicative of a broader lack of fact-based research into what affects student achievement. Over the past two decades, the private sector has made substantial investments in collecting and analysing data. Retailers in the United States know the relationship between the sales of strawberry pop-tarts and the onset of extreme weather (sales of strawberry pop-tarts are more sensitive to hurricane warnings than sales of any other product, with demand rising by a factor of seven immediately before a hurricane).[12] Yet relatively little is known about the relationship between class size and student outcomes, on which decisions about the spending of hundreds of billions of dollars each year depend.

What data does exist suggests that there is a small but significant benefit from reduced class sizes when all other variables are held constant. The biggest experimental study conducted into the effects of class size reduction was the Student Teacher Achievement Ratio project, better known as Project STAR. Between 1985 and 1989, approximately 10,000 students[13] were randomly assigned to one of three classes: a smaller class with around 15 students, a larger class with around 23 students, or a larger class with a teaching aide. Their progress was monitored as they passed through kindergarten and the first three grades of school in one of the types of class.

Overall, the students in the smaller classes achieved a slight performance gain on their peers in the larger classes (the aides made no difference).[14] After four years in the smaller classes, this gain was equivalent to about two months of schooling, or in other words, the students in the smaller classes had learnt in 48 months what the students in the larger classes would have learnt in 50. So while holding all other variables constant in an experimental setting, reducing class sizes from 23 to 15, which would imply hiring 50% more teachers and increasing education spending by about 40%, would have roughly the same effect as extending the school year by ten days.

Another important insight from the STAR data is that most of the gain made by the students in the smaller classes was achieved during kindergarten and the first grade. By the end of the first grade, students in the smaller classes were already two months ahead of their peers in the larger classes. They made no further gains during the remaining two years of the study. This suggests that the benefits of reduced class sizes are found mainly during the first one or two

Figure 3: Test scores in reading (left) and mathematics (right) for small and regular classes during the STAR experiment

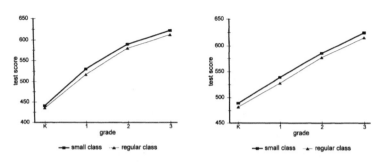

Source: Hanushek, E., "Some Findings from an Independent Investigation" in *Educational Evaluation and Policy Analysis*, 1999.

years of schooling.

The findings of the STAR experiment are consistent with the findings of a smaller experimental study conducted in Toronto during the late 1970s.[15] Students and teachers in grades four and five were randomly assigned to one of four different class sizes, each with either 16, 23, 30, or 37 students, with a total of 62 classes participating. Researchers collected a wide range of data on student academic achievement, development of soft skills, art and self-image, teaching activities, and teacher perceptions of the effects of the class size. They found no effect of class size on any of the measures of student learning, development, or attitudes, with the exception of mathematical concepts, where students in the 16-student classes performed slightly ahead of students in the classes with 30 students or more. There were no differences in students' self-image or attitudes towards school, and no significant variation in teaching practices.

So both the STAR and the Toronto experiments found that reduced class sizes were beneficial, but the benefits were very small, particularly after the age of seven. This finding has been confirmed by a range of other studies and approaches to assessing the impact of class size reduction. Collectively, the research demonstrates that across all school systems, when other variables are held constant, class size either has no effect on outcomes or a very small effect on outcomes. "The large majority of studies have found no significant effects of class size on student achievement. The remainder have shown small benefits, usually only when classes have less than 20 students. [The studies also indicate that] class size has less effect when teachers are competent."[16] A British study concluded that "no evidence was found that students in smaller classes made more progress ... [however] as the size of the class increases, [the] size and number of groups increases, and the management of groups, both in terms of size and number, becomes ever more crucial."[17]

The research also explains why neither of the two major presumed benefits of class size reduction is realized in practice. Smaller classes are presumed to be easier to control, with better behaviour freeing up more time for learning. However, a number of studies show that there is, in fact, little correlation between class size and behaviour, particularly when teachers are competent. Across the developed world, teachers spend about 7% of teaching time maintaining discipline, and there is no relationship between this proportion and class size.[18] Similarly, overall levels of behaviour in schools depend more on the quality of teaching and policies to tackle failure than on the number of students in the classroom. Students who have been consistently failed during primary school are likely to misbehave during secondary school irrespective of the student-to-teacher ratio. At the same time, effective schools and effective teachers are likely to be able to control and sustain the attention of a class of students irrespective of the number of students in that class. Other policy choices also have an impact; for instance, in Singapore and Japan, both of which have relatively large classes, schools compensate for the fact that it is more difficult for a teacher to get to know a larger group of students by assigning teachers to the same set of students for two years in a row (many schools in Scandinavia do this as well, even though their classes are not as large).

The second presumed benefit of smaller classes is that they might allow a greater amount of time for individual instruction. In practice, having smaller classes does not appear to be a good way of individualizing instruction. In California, the research consortium which evaluated the class size reduction initiative found that teaching practices in the smaller classes were almost exactly the same as those in both larger classes and in the same classes prior to class size reduction. In particular, the consortium found that the amount of individual instruction in the reduced classes increased by only seven minutes each day, or approximately 20 seconds for each student. This is despite the fact that all teachers had to participate in professional development programs designed to help them adapt their teaching to the smaller class sizes as a condition for schools to receive the additional funding. Even in a school system where teachers spent one quarter of the school day giving individual instruction, the effect of reducing class size from 30 to 20, a reform which would increase the cost of schooling by around 40%, would be equivalent to extending the school day by 45 minutes.

Most importantly though, all of the studies show that within the range of class sizes typical in developed countries, the effects of class size are completely dominated by the effects of teacher quality. The difference in how much a child learns each year when placed in a small class compared to a large class might be equivalent to one or two weeks of schooling. The difference between how much a child learns each year when placed with an effective teacher compared to an ineffective teacher is equivalent to up to a year of schooling. In other words, the studies show that what really matters is not whether there are 20 students in a classroom or 30 students in a classroom, but whether there is a good teacher in the classroom. That is important, because when class size reduction is implemented across a school system as a whole, it significantly reduces teacher quality.

Reducing class size reduces teacher quality

Every school system has a budget, and the majority of that budget – normally around two thirds of it – is spent on teachers. Each school system then has a choice: it can either have more teachers and spend less money on each one, or it can have fewer teachers and spend more money on each one. That decision drives the level of teacher salaries, which substantially impact who becomes a teacher (discussed further in the next chapter), and it drives the level of spending on supporting and developing each teacher. The policy debate on class size generally casts the issue as a trade-off between higher spending and larger classes (except in Florida, where a class size reduction program was passed into law without any provision for the $3 billion annual cost of the program)[19]. This is in fact misleading; class size reduction is really a three-way trade-off between higher spending, more teachers, and more spending on each teacher.

It is also a trade-off between the number of teachers employed and the selectivity of the teaching profession. Countries with smaller classes need to hire more teachers. As a result, they can be less selective about who becomes a teacher. Singapore and South Korea, which have relatively large class sizes, can turn away 80% of the candidates who apply to enter teacher training, in part, because they need fewer teachers in the first place. This effect is even bigger than it appears for two reasons. First, making entry into the teaching profession more selective and more competitive also raises its status, which in turn attracts even more high-calibre applicants. Conversely, the easier it is to become a teacher, the lower the status of the profession becomes, which in turn drives down the quality and number of applicants to teaching further, and with it the status of the profession. Second, as the number of teachers required increases, the marginal difficulty of attracting each additional teacher also increases. Recruiting 20,000 teachers a year requires more than twice as much effort as recruiting 10,000 teachers a year, because the system needs to attract an additional set of people who are less disposed to becoming a teacher in the first place. Effectively, the price and difficulty of attracting each additional good candidate into the teaching profession increases as the number of teachers required increases (or alternatively, school systems have to accept progressively lower quality).

In California, the class size reduction program meant that the State needed a lot more teachers. In the first two years of the program, the number of teachers in kindergarten through to grade three increased by 38%. As a result, California had to be less selective about who could become a teacher. In 1996, immediately before the reduction, 2% of California's teachers were not fully credentialed, and 17% had less than three years of teaching experience. By 1999, 13% of California's K-3 teachers were not fully credentialed, and almost a third had less than three years of teaching experience. Interestingly, these effects were even more severe in the grades not involved in the class size reduction initiative. The demand for teachers in kindergarten through to grade three meant that more experienced teachers from the upper grades migrated to the lower grades where the new smaller classes meant that they would have a lower workload. As a result, the number of teachers in grades four and five who were not fully credentialed rose from 1% in 1996 to 14% in 1999, while the number of grade four and five teachers with less than three years of teaching experience doubled.

For California, the increased demand for teachers also had significant implications for equity. Schools in high-poverty and high-minority areas which already found it hard to attract sufficient teachers took longer to reduce their class sizes and had to recruit less qualified teachers in order to do so. In many cases, good teachers left schools in low-income areas in order to take up the new teaching positions that had been created by the class size reduction program in high-income areas. In 1999, the proportion of teachers working in schools in high-income areas who were not fully credentialed was still only 3.2%, whereas in low-income areas it had risen to 16%. The official evaluation of the initiative concluded that the class size reduction program "was associated with declines in teacher qualifications and a more inequitable distribution of credentialed teachers."[20]

Three caveats

These findings should not lead to the conclusion that having very large class sizes would be a good strategy for a school system. Clearly, there must be a point at which the benefits of having smaller classes outweigh the benefits of higher teacher quality. Very large classes might also deter people from becoming teachers, although the research shows that the effect of class size on attracting and retaining teachers is much less than the effect of the corresponding salary increase made possible by larger class sizes.[21] Unfortunately, the research that would give us a sufficient understanding of the relationships between class size, teaching, and student development to allow us to determine where that tipping point might be has not yet been carried out, except to say that it is at a point larger than the class size tolerated by almost all of the developed world's schools. In some circumstances, teaching can still be effective with extremely large class sizes. One particularly talented mathematics teacher in South Africa regularly teaches classes of more than one thousand students to great effect. Other data from Africa suggest that in most cases there is a tipping point where learning is impacted when class size exceeds 60 students,[22] but that conclusion probably would not apply in other circumstances.

There are two other important caveats to the conclusion that smaller classes lead to lower performance. The first is that within school systems, schools with smaller classes sometimes show stronger performance than schools with larger classes. In the United States for instance, states with smaller class sizes frequently perform better than those with larger class sizes. There are a range of reasons why this happens. Often, it reflects the fact that schools in more wealthy areas are better funded and use some of that extra funding to reduce class sizes. The schools perform better overall, though that higher performance is a consequence of the backgrounds of the students they serve, not their smaller class sizes. Sometimes, schools in low-income areas are unable to attract enough teachers, and therefore have larger classes. Again, their lower level of performance is not the result of the larger classes, but the fact that they serve more disadvantaged students and attract less-qualified teachers. In California, during the first year of the class size reduction, about half of the State's students were in small classes. These students performed better than those still in larger classes by a significant margin. However, the effect was almost entirely attributable to the fact that schools in high-income areas had been able to recruit the extra teachers required to reduce class sizes more quickly, often by taking them from schools in low-income areas. Once the effect of student background was accounted for, the performance gap between the smaller and larger classes disappeared.

The final caveat is that there are some cases where small classes, even very small classes, can be highly effective. Chapter eight explores different interventions to support students who are falling behind at school. Among them, providing the lowest-performing students with intensive tuition in very small groups, often fewer than five students, can be pivotal in ensuring that they overcome obstacles to learning and make progress. Dividing large classes into smaller groups is often essential to ensure that all students are able to learn, particularly when classes span a wide range of abilities. However, the fact that there are specific cases where small group teaching can be desirable or even essential is not an argument for uniform reductions in class size.

Student-to-teacher ratios explain much of the variation in the performance of different school systems

So within the range of class sizes typical of developed countries, smaller classes, in and of themselves, have only a small impact on student achievement, equivalent at most to extending the school year by two weeks. However, having smaller classes implies having lower quality teachers, because school systems can be less selective about who becomes a teacher, and can spend less money on each teacher at any given funding level. Essentially therefore, class size reduction implies a trade-off between two variables: the number of students in each classroom (which does not matter very much), and the quality of teachers (which matters enormously). These findings are borne out by the international data on student performance: school systems which employ fewer teachers have stronger student performance, and this one variable explains more of the variation in performance between school systems than any other policy choice. Overall, student-to-teacher ratios explain almost 40% of the variation in performance of developed country school systems on international tests.[23]

This finding that class size reduction can reduce overall performance also helps to explain the lack of improvement in many school

Figure 4: Student to teacher ratio and average score in PISA for OECD countries

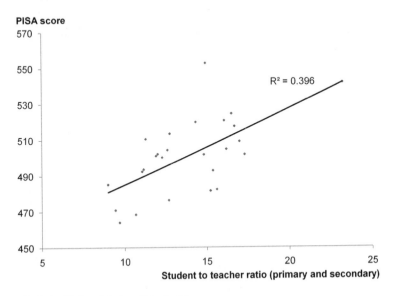

*Excludes Turkey, Mexico, Canada, Norway
Source: *PISA 2006*; OECD

systems over the past four decades. Since the late 1960s, most school systems have been trading in teacher quality for smaller classes. In the United States, for instance, average class size fell dramatically between 1971 and 2001. Though spending on schools also increased, it did not keep pace with the combined effect of larger numbers of teachers and greater spending on non-teacher costs. As a result, average teacher salaries relative to GDP per capita fell by almost one third. This pattern of increasing numbers of teachers accompanied by a fall in relative salaries is repeated for every region in the world, both developed and developing.[24] It suggests that teacher quality has been falling over the past three decades, and partly explains why there has been little improvement in the performance of schools despite so many attempts to reform.

It also suggests that policies to attract and select the right people to become teachers are important. If student-to-teacher ratios are

Figure 5: Teacher numbers and salaries in the United States

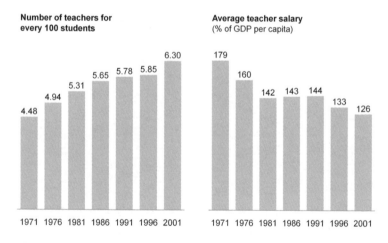

Number of teachers for every 100 students

4.48   4.94   5.31   5.65   5.78   5.85   6.30

Average teacher salary (% of GDP per capita)

179   160   142   143   144   133   126

1971 1976 1981 1986 1991 1996 2001

Source: National Center for Education Statistics

important because of the effect they have on the quality of people who enter teaching, then other policies influencing the quality of people entering teaching are also likely to be important. The next chapter examines those.

3.

How Finland
came top in PISA

(Getting the right people to become teachers)

The performance of a school system rests on the quality of its teachers. School systems which have made teaching an attractive career choice and are selective about who becomes a teacher tend to be among the top-performing school systems in the world. The best school systems have five or six applicants for every place in teacher training and rigorously select those with the right attributes to become effective teachers. Many policymakers attribute the attractiveness of a career in teaching to variables seemingly outside their control: among them culture, the status of the teaching profession, and the government's willingness to pay ever higher teacher salaries. In fact, getting the right people to become teachers depends more on a simple set of policy choices: rigorously selecting applicants before they enter teacher training, opening up different routes into teaching, paying good compensation, and actively promoting teaching careers.

The teaching profession in Finland
Every three years, the OECD runs a series of tests known as PISA. PISA tests 15-year olds in mathematics, science, reading, and problem solving, and is designed to help policymakers understand how students and schools are performing in different school systems. The tests are now taken by representative samples of students in almost 70 countries and give us a unique and valuable set of insights into how different schools are performing and why.

When the results of the first PISA assessments were released on

6 December 2001, the country with the highest scores in the tests, as in every round of testing since, was Finland. Not only do Finnish students score higher in the tests, the PISA data also show that they read more books, visit libraries more often, like school more, and have better relationships with their teachers than students in other countries. They also spend less time in school. Finnish children do not start school until they reach the age of seven, and even when they do start school, they spend only three to four hours in classes each day. However, for every hour that they spend in the classroom, Finnish children learn more than children in almost any other school system, and with an astonishingly high level of reliability: there is almost no variation in the effectiveness of different schools in Finland, and the effect of a child's background on how they perform at school is weaker than in almost any other OECD country.[1]

Back in December 2001, the Finnish success in PISA came as something of a surprise, not least of all to the Finns.[2] As Andreas Schleicher, Director of the PISA program, notes: "[At the time] few people were looking to Finland when it comes to education; that's not necessarily because Finland did not do well in the 1990s, but perhaps simply because we did not know."[3] Moreover, there were few obvious explanations for the success. Finland spends less on students in its schools than most other developed countries, and much less than its neighbours. The other Scandinavian countries, several of which had participated in earlier international tests, do not have particularly strong records of school performance: Norway, Sweden, Denmark, and Iceland generally perform close to the developed country average. Though Finland does have a relatively homogeneous and stable population, analysis of the country performance data suggests that this explains only a small part of its performance on PISA. The opening line of a Finnish research publication written to try and explain the results sums up the conundrum well when it states that: "The outstanding success of Finnish students in PISA has been a great joy but at the same time a somewhat puzzling experience to all those responsible for and making decisions about education in Finland."[4]

One thing however which does distinguish Finland from most other school systems is that it has been remarkably successful at attracting and selecting people to become teachers. More than one quarter of young people in Finland rate teaching as their top career choice.[5] Applications to enter teacher training colleges at universities massively exceed the number of available places:[6] in Helsinki, there are 15 applications for every place in teacher training (this compares well to MIT in the United States, with an average of 8.6 applicants for every place, Caltech with 5.6, or the University of Oxford with 3.2). Across the country as a whole, there are 6.7 applicants for every place in undergraduate teacher training.[7] The status of the teaching profession is high, and there are few signs of that status falling over time.

Once applicants have applied to teacher training, there is a rigorous selection process to identify those with the strongest potential and aptitude for teaching. It starts with a national test of numeracy, literacy, and problem solving which ensures that all entrants to teacher training are highly educated and literate, and also provides a national standard in a process which is otherwise controlled by the individual universities responsible for teacher training. Applicants with the highest scores on the test move on to a series of exercises consisting of interviews, group work, essays, and assessment days designed to test soft skills and motivation to become a teacher. Some universities ask applicants to complete work experience in a school before being offered a place. The process ensures that entrants to the profession have the right intrinsics to become effective teachers, and its rigour in turn helps to keep the status and attractiveness of the profession high. The number of places is controlled both to ensure that graduates from teacher training are able to find a teaching position upon completion of their courses, and to keep entry into the courses as competitive as possible.

Importantly, the choices that have enabled Finland to consistently attract and select good candidates into teaching are remarkably similar to those made in Singapore, which tops the other main international comparisons of student performance.[8] Their choices are also remarkably similar to those made by a series of innovative programs designed to get top graduates to become teachers in the United States and England.

Getting top graduates to choose teaching: Teach First and Teach For America

Teach First, a charity based in London's Canary Wharf, began recruiting graduates from Britain's top universities in 2002. In its first year, it recruited 186 graduates,[9] trained them to teach through a six-week summer course combined with coaching and mentoring during their first years of teaching, and placed them into some of the most challenging secondary schools in London. They were expected to teach in those schools for two years, after which Teach First would help them find jobs in leading businesses, though half in fact chose to stay on in teaching at the end of their first two years. Six years later in 2008, the program had tripled in size and expanded from London to Manchester and the Midlands, and was on course to become the biggest recruiter and trainer of new teachers in the United Kingdom. When final-year university students in British universities were asked "which employer offers the best opportunities for graduates," they ranked Teach First 14th, ahead of leading graduate employers such as BP, Citigroup, Google, Microsoft, and UBS.[10]

Teach First was inspired by a similar program started in the United States in 1990. Its founder and creator, Wendy Kopp, imagined a program that would "make teaching an attractive choice for top graduates by surrounding it with an aura of status and selectivity, streamlining the process of applying for teaching positions, and assuring recent graduates a job and a steady income."[11] Teach For America has steadily expanded and refined its recruitment, selection, and training processes, currently recruits 4,000 graduates each year, and is ranked the 10th best employer in the United States in surveys of final-year university students.[12]

Both Teach For America and Teach First aim to recruit, train, and place top graduates into challenging schools. They use careful marketing and branding, systematic promotion, links to the private sector, and the option to get straight into the classroom without spending a year in teacher training to make the program attractive to graduates who would not otherwise consider entering teaching. They use rigorous selection processes, including a full-day assessment centre, to ensure that they select people with the right skills and attributes to be highly effective teachers.[13] The rigour of the selection process – both programs typically accept less than one applicant in five – itself contributes to making the program an attractive high-status option. The support and mentoring of teachers during their first two years teaching ensures that they develop the skills they need to be effective in the classroom, and as a result makes them less likely to become frustrated or demoralized as a result of feeling unable to cope with the challenges they face in schools and classrooms.

In 2007, an independent evaluation of participants in the Teach First program by the government's education inspectors rated them among the best new teachers produced by any teacher training route, despite having had far less formal training than entrants to teaching through other routes. "Around half achieved the [standard for becoming a teacher] to an outstanding level, a third to a good level and the others to a satisfactory level. ... Four of the trainees seen during visits to schools were judged by inspectors to be amongst the most exceptional trainees produced by any teacher training route. ... At least one of the schools visited attributed a rapid improvement in its standards almost entirely to the contribution of Teach First participants."[14] Participants in the Teach For America program have also been found to be more effective than teachers trained on conventional routes.[15] Moreover, both programs aspire to have a wider impact on the school system as a whole by bringing a new generation of leaders into education. Several hundred former Teach For America participants now run their own schools.[16] A few are leading entire school systems through ambitious reforms. KIPP, the network of highly successful schools described in the first chapter, was established by two former Teach For America participants. The model developed by Teach For America and Teach First is now spreading to other countries, with teams working to launch similar programs in Chile, Estonia, Germany, India, Israel, Latvia, Lebanon, Lithuania, and South Africa.[17]

Why getting the right people to become teachers matters

Research on the characteristics of effective teachers shows that although they are a diverse and eclectic group, they tend to share a set of common characteristics.[18] They believe that all children can succeed and are highly committed to ensuring that they do. They are able to form excellent working relationships with children and adults. They have good pedagogical and communication skills and are able to draw on a wide range of teaching strategies and techniques. They are critical of their own practice and reflect on ways to improve it. They are well educated and highly achieving themselves. They tend to have high literacy and numeracy scores, and a good knowledge of the subject they teach. Most importantly, they are passionate about teaching, and about teaching as well as they can.

Some of those characteristics are the product of good training and development, while others depend on the school context and culture in which teachers work; a culture of high expectations, for instance, can be introduced into a school by an excellent principal.[19]

However, many are characteristics which depend on attracting and selecting the right people in the first place. Research evidence from the United States shows that even if a group of teachers have received the same training, and work in the same school with the same curriculum, there will still be massive differences in their individual effectiveness.[20] Those differences reflect the importance of individual attributes to becoming a great teacher, and more generally, the importance of getting the right people to become teachers to creating an effective school system.

Unsurprisingly, those school systems which have made teaching an attractive career choice and are selective about who becomes a teacher tend to outperform those which are not. Finland, South Korea, Singapore, Cuba, and some parts of Canada all have at least five applicants for every teacher training position. In all of them, teaching is rated highly as a profession by high-school graduates and the quality of applicants is high. In Finland and South Korea, entrants into teaching are typically among the top five to ten percent of high-school graduates. Both countries score top in the world on international tests despite having implemented few of the other reforms which would normally lead to high performance in schools.

Conversely, school systems which are less selective about who becomes a teacher generally achieve little more than average performance, even if their school system is well run in most other ways. England has implemented more of the policies which would be expected to improve performance in a school system than any other country in the world.[21] However, it is not selective about who becomes a teacher, with fewer than 1.2 applicants for every position in teacher training, a low minimum standard for entry to teacher training, and an admissions process which tends to admit candidates with high exam scores irrespective of their aptitude for teaching.[22] Its overall performance at age 15 is little above the average for developed countries. School systems which are the least selective about who becomes a teacher also tend to be the lowest performing. Israel, the lowest performing developed country in the PISA assessments, has lower starting salaries for teachers relative to GDP per capita than any OECD country, and a corresponding struggle to attract talent to the profession.[23]

Culture, status, and the five policies that make teaching attractive

Yet if there is a consensus among policymakers that making teaching an attractive career choice is important, there is also a strong belief that transforming the status of teaching is a challenging, if not impossible, undertaking. The attractiveness of the profession is often regarded as something outside the control of the policymaker; the product of culture, the status of teachers in society, or, at best, the willingness of central government to pay ever higher teacher salaries. Commentators claim that the Asian and Scandinavian countries which have succeeded in making teaching an attractive career choice have done so mainly because their societies have a unique and irreplicable tendency to respect and value teachers, while some western school leaders claim that there is little they can do to improve the attractiveness of teaching when society as a whole views it as a low-status option.

In practice, the role of cultural and social factors in determining the attractiveness of the teaching profession seems to be overstated. There is no consistent relationship between culture and the status of the teaching profession. Teaching is a top career choice in Cuba and Finland, but not in other Latin American, Scandinavian, or Baltic countries. In Asia, teaching is the most popular career choice among young people in South Korea, but ranks 17th in Japan[24] and struggles to attract good candidates in the Philippines.[25] Teach First and Teach For America demonstrate that a shift in the status of teaching among potential applicants can be achieved in a relatively short time, without a corresponding shift in broader cultural attitudes towards education. One evaluation of the Teach First program noted that it had "succeeded in making teaching acceptable among a group who had perceived it as having low status ... by constructing the participants as an elite group."[26] This is not to say that there is no effect of culture on the status of the teaching profession but, rather, that over the long term that effect appears to be small compared to the impact of policy.

However, even if they are not long-term drivers of the attractiveness of the teaching profession, status and culture do constitute powerful inertial forces. Countries which have historically made teaching an attractive and selective career choice should have a highly capable and well respected teaching cadre as a result. That in turn makes it easier to attract more talent into the teaching profession, which then makes it easier to maintain the high status and attractiveness of the profession. As a result of those effects, countries like Finland and Singapore can pay lower salaries to teachers and still attract more talented applicants than school systems in other countries. Conversely, countries which have historically recruited less able graduates into teaching, and therefore have a less well respected profession, will find it more difficult to attract excellent candidates, even if they apply a similar set of policies and pay higher salaries.

Nonetheless, a range of school systems prove that, irrespective of culture, teaching can become a top career choice, and that substantial changes in the attractiveness of the teaching profession can be achieved in a short period of time. The first part of getting the right people to become teachers, discussed in the previous chapter, is to have fewer teachers. Countries like Singapore and South Korea are able to make entry into teaching selective, in part, because they need roughly half as many teachers as other school systems in the first place.[27] However, beyond having fewer teachers, school systems can do four other things to improve the status, attractiveness and selectivity of the teaching profession:

Figure 6: Ensuring that the right people become teachers

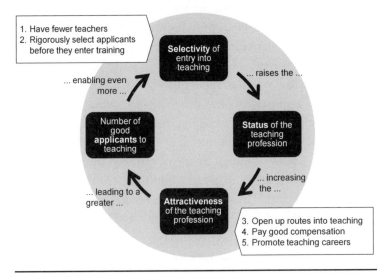

- rigorously select applicants before they enter teacher training;
- open up different routes into teaching;
- pay good compensation; and
- actively promote careers in teaching.

Rigorously selecting applicants before they enter teacher training

How school systems select applicants for teacher training and teaching positions has an obvious effect on who becomes a teacher through the choice of selection criteria and processes that are used, and also a less obvious but equally important effect through the impact that those selection processes have on the perception of the teaching profession and the employment prospects of new teachers. The combination of those effects explains much of the variation in the quality of new teachers and the attractiveness of the teaching profession between different school systems.

Many school systems set very low requirements for entry into teacher training. In Germany anybody who has graduated from an academic high school has the right to enter and remain in teacher training, irrespective of their aptitude or suitability for teaching (unsurprisingly German research suggests that less than a third of those enrolled in teacher training have the intrinsics to become effective teachers). In a few countries, applicants who have been rejected from other courses at university, often due to poor academic performance, are offered places on teacher training courses instead. In Greece, for instance, only 15% of people enrolling on primary teacher training courses had actually chosen it as one of their top three preferences for study at university.[28] In several Middle Eastern school systems, the majority of teacher trainees are both among the lowest performing high-school graduates to enter university, and enrolled in teacher training because they have been placed there by the university rather than because they want to become teachers.[29] In those systems, it is difficult to believe either that the majority of the candidates in teacher training have the intrinsics to become effective teachers, or that teacher training and, by implication, teaching could ever become an attractive high-status choice.

In other countries, requirements and processes to control entry into teaching and teacher training are in place, but prove ineffective, either because they select based on the wrong criteria, because they use the wrong methods to test those criteria, or because they set the bar too low. For instance, under federal legislation passed in the United States in 2002, public schools are generally only allowed to employ teachers who are 'certified' by the state. Certification requirements vary, but in general they require prospective teachers to take a series of tests of subject knowledge, numeracy, and literacy, and to complete a teacher training program.

The problem is that none of the things tested in the certification process are particularly good predictors of future teaching ability. For instance, people with higher scores on numeracy and literacy tests tend to perform better in the classroom,[30] but the correlation is weak: not everybody with high numeracy and literacy scores will be a good teacher, and there are some people with average scores who make excellent teachers. Similarly, though basic subject knowledge is important, there is little evidence that teachers with a deeper knowledge of the subject they teach make better teachers,[31] and much evidence that somebody with a deep knowledge of a subject will not necessarily be a good teacher of it. Moreover, in many cases, the tests of numeracy, literacy, and subject knowledge used during the certification process are too easy to be an effective test of real ability. Finally, though good teacher training programs can produce more effective teachers, many school systems have found that teachers who have completed existing teacher training courses perform little better than those who have not.[32] Unsurprisingly, studies of certification find that, overall, certified teachers perform no better in the classroom than teachers who have not been certified, or at best, the difference is marginal.[33]

The negative effects of poor selection processes are often compounded by the fact that school systems allow too many people to enter teacher training. In many countries, teacher training programs accept between two and four times as many candidates as are actually required by the system. This unnecessary lack of selectivity has a series of effects. It pushes down the status of the courses and makes them unattractive to those with the option to enter more selective programs. The quality of the training falls, both because the resources available are spread over a larger number of students, and because the people on the courses are likely to be less capable and less committed. The probability that graduates will find employment in teaching is reduced, because there is an oversupply of teacher trainees, while at the same time, their chances of finding employment in other areas falls because the courses they have taken are perceived as markers of low ability by other employers. The combined effect of low requirements for entry into teacher training and having too many people on the courses makes it even more difficult to attract high-performing graduates into teacher training, and by implication, into the teaching profession as a whole.

The effects of allowing too many people to enter teacher training are most strongly visible in South Korea. South Korea pays very high salaries to teachers, guarantees them a job for life, and has for a long time had a teaching profession which is well regarded by society as a whole. Unsurprisingly, teaching is a highly attractive career choice. Training of new primary teachers is carefully controlled, with strict limits on the number of places available. As a result, admission has become highly selective: successful applicants are typically in the top 5% of their academic cohort, and the status of the courses is extremely high.

In contrast, the number of training places for secondary school teachers is not controlled. Because of attractive job conditions, demand for teacher training is high, and the number of places on teacher training has expanded. There are now eleven qualified graduates from secondary teacher training for every teaching post. This oversupply has pushed down the status, quality, and attractiveness of the courses, reduced the quality of new secondary teachers, and has begun to deter high-calibre candidates from entering secondary teacher training.[34] Some South Korean policymakers argue that a widespread public belief that the primary school system is much stronger than the secondary school system is almost entirely attributable to this one policy choice.

Those school systems which have been successful in making teaching both attractive and selective share a number of features. First, they design processes and criteria which are closely linked to the characteristics of successful teachers, and then apply them rigorously and consistently during selection processes. Designing a good selection process (like those used by Finland, Singapore, Teach

First and Teach For America) is difficult, because most of the attributes which suggest that somebody will make an excellent teacher are difficult to measure, while those attributes which are easy to measure tend to be bad predictors of future teaching ability.[35] No process will be perfect, but those school systems appear to have found selection methods which do produce consistently better teachers. Even where they are not able to precisely predict who will be a good teacher, the rigour of their processes both maintains the high status of the teacher training programs and ensures that new teachers are sufficiently talented to be able to find jobs elsewhere if they prove less effective once they enter the classroom. Teach For America deliberately made it difficult to get onto the program in order to make it attractive to high-performing graduates. As Wendy Kopp recalls of Teach For America's first interview process, "it was the following question that may have done more than any other to shape our image on campus: '(1) What is wind? Don't describe it, just tell me what it is. (2) Phenomenologists draw an analogy between religion and the wind, claiming that one can't see religion, only the manifestations of it – like synagogues, churches, and mosques. Similarly, one can't see wind, only manifestations of it – waves in a wheat field, mobbing branches. What other analogy can you draw to the wind?' Looking back, I have to laugh at the thought of our recruiters asking this question of every applicant. But it created the desired effect. Teach For America was clearly not something for the intellectually meek."[36]

Equally importantly, they limit the number of places on teacher training so that it exactly matches the requirements of the system, thereby making entry into teacher training as selective as possible. Raising the requirements for entry into teacher training has both an immediate effect on raising the quality of new teachers, by reducing the number of people on the courses and removing those who are unlikely to become effective teachers, and a long-term effect by raising the status of teacher training and by extension the profession as a whole. It means that the minimum number of people are admitted to teacher training, allowing the system to spend more on each person in training. It keeps the quality of courses high, because the people on them are carefully selected and more committed (more than 85% of graduates from teacher training are expected to become teachers in Finland and Singapore, compared to less than one third in some OECD countries), and it makes the programs more attractive by increasing the chances that graduates will find a job either inside or outside education. In both Finland and Singapore, unlike in many other countries, teachers find it relatively easy to start new careers outside education, because their training is seen as a mark of high ability rather than as a signal of low prior achievement.

Unfortunately, raising the requirements to enter teacher training without enacting other policies to increase the attractiveness of the teaching profession is risky because of the possibility that those higher requirements may lead to a shortage of teachers. Interestingly, this is not necessarily the case; Chicago, for instance, found that raising the requirements to enter teaching produced an increase in the number of candidates, for precisely the reasons described above. Ironically, when faced with a shortage of teachers, most governments respond by lowering requirements for entry into teaching,[37] which tends to produce a fall in the number of good applicants in the long term. However, in most cases, raising the requirements to enter teacher training needs to be complemented by other measures to raise the number of applicants relative to the number of teachers required. One option is to have fewer teachers. Others involve raising the attractiveness of the profession by other means.

Opening up multiple routes into teaching
In most school systems, people who want to become teachers first need to complete teacher training at a university or college of higher

education. Most countries allow people to do this in one (or often both) of two ways: either through a three to four-year undergraduate program, or through a one or two-year postgraduate program. The problem with both of these models is that they place severe limits on the pool of people who can become teachers. When a country only offers the first option – to become a teacher by studying on a four-year undergraduate program – the pool of people who can become teachers is effectively limited to those people who have already decided to become teachers at the age of 18. People who want to keep their options open, or do not know what they want to do, or want to do something else first, are effectively excluded from teaching. This problem is particularly severe in lower-performing education systems, where few talented school leavers are likely to commit to a lifetime career in teaching at the beginning of their university studies. In the United States, for instance, students who choose teacher education as their preferred major when taking the SAT examination have some of the lowest SAT scores of all students planning to go to college.[38]

Even in those countries which offer the option to qualify as a teacher through a shorter one or two year postgraduate course, those courses still severely constrain the pool of potential applicants.[39] People joining them have to accept a substantial financial loss: they lose the income they could have earned in another job in addition to having to pay the costs of study and living during the course (except in a few countries like Singapore, which covers the costs of training and pays a full salary during the course). There is generally no guarantee that they will find a job as a teacher at the end of their course, and having a teaching qualification may harm their chances of finding another job if that qualification carries a low status. "For more mature career changes, the risk is even greater if they have a family to support and other financial commitments."[40] As a result, many candidates are likely to be deterred, particularly those who have other good options in the job market.

In a few high-performing education systems, where teaching already enjoys a high and stable status, these problems are likely to be less significant. Because teacher training courses are well-respected, and graduates find it easy to gain employment in other fields after graduation if they choose to do so, it should be possible for the system to attract a sufficiently large number of high-quality applicants to make this the main route into teaching. This is the case in Cuba, Finland, South Korea, and Singapore. In these countries, the longer teacher training courses have the benefit of providing new teachers with a strong foundation for future teaching and also contribute to maintaining the status of the profession. However, most countries will not be able to attract a sufficiently large number of high-quality candidates through these courses, and even those which can lose many good potential teachers as a result.

One way of overcoming this problem is to create additional routes into teaching. These programs allow people, typically career changers from other professions, to start teaching in a school with just a few weeks of training, and then complete their teacher training on-the-job during their first two years. Examples include the Boston Teacher Residency, the Chicago and New York Teaching Fellows, the Graduate Teacher Programme in England, and school-based training in the Netherlands, in addition to Teach First and Teach For America. These programs have been introduced based on a recognition that getting the best people to become teachers matters more than ensuring that they attend a long teacher training program, as long as the shorter training is of a high quality.

Countries which have opened up these routes into teaching have been able to increase both the number and quality of applicants as a result. England, for instance, introduced employment-based routes into teaching in 1998. Enrolment on these routes expanded from 100 in the first year[41] to more than 7,000 in 2006, accounting for

22% of new teachers.[42] A large proportion of these, including a disproportionately large number of men, had worked in another profession for more than five years before entering teacher training. Official evaluations found that these teachers were better qualified, more motivated, and stronger teachers after their first two years of teaching than those who had entered the profession by traditional routes; a finding common to similar programs in other countries. They were also more likely to be male, non-white, over 30, and intend to remain in teaching for at least five years.[43] So opening up additional routes into teaching appears to increase not only the number and quality of applicants, but also the diversity of the teaching workforce.

Paying good compensation

The next part of getting the right people to become teachers is paying good compensation. Numerous research studies demonstrate that both the number and quality of applicants to teaching is strongly related to the salaries teachers are paid, particularly their starting salaries.[44] Israel, Estonia, and Latvia,[45] with some of the lowest teacher salaries in the developed world, all struggle to attract talented applicants. Conversely, rises in teacher salaries are associated with larger numbers of applicants: in England, for instance, a 10% increase in relative teacher salaries is associated with a 30% rise in applications to teaching. Focus groups in the United States suggest that half of all college students would consider a career in teaching if salaries were increased by 20%.[46]

Importantly, the level of starting salaries appears to matter more than average compensation over the course of a career, and as a result, the way in which school systems structure compensation has a significant effect on their ability to attract good teachers. The following graph demonstrates two different approaches to setting salary scales for teachers. On the first line – the steep salary scale – salaries

Figure 7: Salary scales for teachers

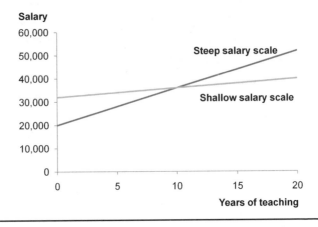

start at a low level, but then rise relatively steeply over the course of a teaching career. This pattern is generally found in North America, the Middle East, and many developing countries. In the second, salaries start at a much higher level, but then there is a relatively small rise over the course of a teaching career. This pattern is typical in Finland, Singapore, and Australia. Both scales ultimately end up giving teachers the same overall pay over the course of their career, and both cost the school system the same amount of money over time. However, they have very different implications for who becomes and remains a teacher.

With a steep salary scale schools are less able to attract good candidates because early salaries have a much bigger effect on the decision to become a teacher than the prospects of salary growth, particularly among those who are not certain when they enter teaching that they will dedicate their full career to working in education.[47] Then, having attracted fewer of the good candidates, schools are more likely to retain people who do not enjoy or are not good at teaching because the salary structure encourages them to stay. In

contrast, school systems which opt for the second scale reverse this
state of affairs. They attract better candidates initially because early
salaries are good, and are likely to retain only those who enjoy teaching because the salary structure offers less pecuniary incentive to stay
in the system. These policies are justified in part by evidence that
teacher quality does not tend to improve much with experience, except during the first few years as new teachers develop basic teaching
skills.[48] Some countries have managed to achieve the same effect of
paying a higher salary to new teachers by other means, for instance
by paying training bursaries and signing bonuses to new teachers (as
in England) or by paying a salary during initial teacher training (as
in Singapore).

The overall effect of salary levels, particularly early salary levels,
on the performance of a school system is significant. The graph on
the following page shows the performance in PISA of each of the
OECD countries on the vertical axis and the average salary of teachers during their first few years of teaching (relative to GDP per
capita) on the horizontal axis. Overall, early-career salaries can explain around one quarter of the variation in performance of different
developed country school systems in PISA, with school systems
which pay higher early salaries having stronger overall performance.[49]
The chart is remarkably similar to the chart in the previous chapter
comparing PISA results with student-to-teacher ratios, and clearly
the two are linked: school systems with fewer teachers also tend to
pay higher starting salaries. The most extreme example of this effect
is South Korea (at the far right of the graph), which maintains high
student-to-teacher ratios and large class sizes in order to reduce the
number of teachers it requires. As a result it is able to pay salaries
which are more than double the developed country average. Not
only do teachers' salaries start very high, they also rise quickly, more
than doubling by the end of a teaching career.

The effect of teacher salaries on the quality and quantity of ap-

Figure 8: Early-career teacher salaries and average score in PISA for OECD countries

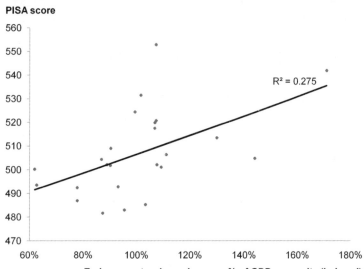

PISA score

R² = 0.275

Early-career teacher salary as a % of GDP per capita (indexed)

Source: *PISA 2006*, OECD

plicants to teaching is even more striking when comparing teachers of different school subjects. The graph opposite shows how much graduates from British universities with degrees in different subjects earn over their lifetime compared to people who graduate from school but do not go to university. Graduates in science and mathematics earn almost one quarter of a million pounds more over their lifetime than the average school graduate who did not go to university. Graduates of arts and humanities, on the other hand, earn only £40,000 more than a school graduate over the course of their careers.

However, despite the fact that graduates with degrees in different subjects can earn very different amounts in the job market, teachers of science, mathematics, arts, and humanities in the United Kingdom are all paid according to the same salary scale. Unsurprisingly, there are much greater shortages of teachers in subjects like mathematics and science, where qualified candidates can earn much more in the job market, than there are in subjects like the humanities where degree holders earn much less. The quality of candidates is also much lower.[50] For instance, 71% of graduates training to teach history have a 2:1 or better in their first degree, compared to 42% of graduates training to teach mathematics. These patterns are repeated across the entire developed world. All of the OECD's school systems pay similar salaries to teachers regardless of the subject that they teach,[51] and as a result, all of them face relative shortages of teachers in subjects where average graduate salaries are high, while they face relative surpluses in subjects where graduate salaries are low.[52] Even in Finland, where the teaching profession consistently enjoys a very high status and large numbers of applicants, there is

Figure 9: Additional lifetime earnings by degree subject (United Kingdom; compared to two or more A-Levels)

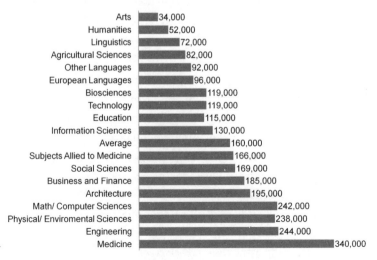

Source: Price Waterhouse Coopers, *The Economic Benefits of a Degree*, 2007

concern about the supply of mathematics and science teachers.[53] More generally, the data shows that how teacher salaries compare to salaries in other professions has a significant impact on the number and quality of applicants.

However, despite that evidence, the importance of teacher salaries can be overstated. Finland, Italy, Australia, and New Zealand have similar student-to-teacher ratios, and similar levels of compensation for beginning teachers, yet Finland attracts far more applicants for every position in teacher training than the others. In England, most applicants to Teach First say that they would not have applied to become teachers through a regular teacher recruitment process, even though the salaries they are paid, the job they do, and the schools they work in are exactly the same. Moreover, countries with high salaries for teachers do not necessarily get the best applicants.[54] Importantly, the benefits of paying higher salaries appear only to be realised when entry into teacher training is made selective.[55] So while making entry into teaching selective and raising early salaries can have a powerful effect on the system in combination, either policy would likely have a much more limited effect if implemented on its own.

Actively promoting careers in teaching

The final part of getting the right people to become teachers is actively promoting careers in teaching. Promoting teaching will generally do little to improve the number or quality of applicants if the profession is fundamentally unattractive as a career choice. Advertisers in the private sector have long recognized that even the best branding and marketing will not produce sustained high sales of an overpriced product. However, efforts to promote careers in teaching can be highly successful when combined with policies which make entry into teaching attractive and selective.

In late 2000, a shortage of new teachers in England provoked a political crisis over the attractiveness of the teaching profession. A survey showed that when undergraduates and young people were asked what job they would like to do next, teaching ranked 96th. In response, the agency responsible for teacher training launched a highly effective set of initiatives to increase the attractiveness of a career in teaching. They increased salaries, started paying signing bonuses to teachers of subjects where the shortage was greatest, and introduced training bursaries to help support those in teacher training. They opened up new routes into teaching to attract more career changers and ran a series of initiatives to attract teachers from other countries.

These efforts were accompanied by a massive marketing campaign aimed at raising the status of the profession and publicising the new benefits. An Academy Award winning producer was hired to develop a series of television commercials promoting teaching, which were complemented by a print and media campaign. Advertisements were carefully designed based on an emerging understanding of what messages most appealed to prospective teachers. Research showed that the main attraction of a career in teaching was helping children to learn, but that many people were deterred from applying by the perception that pay was low. Advertising was designed with both of these insights in mind; it combined images which captured the impact that new teachers could have on children's learning with details of the new pay packages. A national information line was set up for those interested in teaching. Callers to the number were screened to assess whether they were likely to be able to enter teaching, and then high-potential candidates were targeted with additional marketing and support. Within five years, teaching ranked first as a career choice among graduates and young people.[56]

Getting the right people to become teachers is fundamental to improving teaching and learning, and appears to account for between one third and one half of the variation in the performance of different school systems. However, many schools have massively improved their performance without changing any of their teaching staff. Some school systems have achieved substantial improvement across the system with broadly the same workforce. In the business sector, corporate transformations frequently occur without substantial changes in staffing. The challenge for most school systems, therefore, is to help their existing teaching force become as effective as possible. The remaining chapters discuss different ways of doing that.

4.

An unusual ability to
achieve extraordinary results

(Ensuring that every school has effective leadership)

How well teachers teach and how well students learn depends greatly on the quality of the schools they teach and learn in. Excellent school leaders create schools in which teachers and students who might struggle elsewhere can perform to a high standard. They set high expectations, create an environment in which students and teachers are supported to achieve them, and carefully manage teaching, learning, and improvement. Their effect is substantial: student achievement in a school almost never exceeds the quality of its leadership and management, and improvements in performance almost never occur in the absence of good leadership. Ensuring that every school has excellent leadership means doing four things: creating the right programs to apprentice and develop school leaders, attracting and selecting the right people for leadership positions, empowering leaders and protecting their time, and intervening quickly to tackle ineffective school leadership.

Student achievement in a school almost never exceeds the quality of its leadership and management

Every three years, schools in England are inspected by an independent government agency called Ofsted. Ofsted is responsible for monitoring and reporting on the quality of education in England, and reports directly to parliament through a chief inspector. It was originally established as Her Majesty's Inspectorate for Schools under Queen Victoria in 1839 in response to the establishment of similar agencies in Prussia and the Netherlands, countries which were, at the time, perceived to be ahead of England in developing their school systems (by 2006, England had caught up with modern-day Germany, but still lags behind the Netherlands). Modern inspections rate schools on a range of criteria including student achievement, the quality of teaching, safety, student behaviour, and others, and are intended to provide schools with an objective assessment of their performance, make school leadership accountable for improvement, and give parents and the public an independent assessment of school quality.

One by-product of the inspection system is an unrivalled database of information on the performance of individual schools. That database shows that, at least in England, student achievement in a school almost never exceeds the quality of its leadership and management. For every 100 schools that have good leadership and management, 93 will have good standards of achievement. For every 100 schools that do not have good leadership and management, only 1 will have good standards of student achievement. As early as the 1970s, an official Ofsted report noted that good schools "differ in very many respects as institutions, although each can demonstrate quality in its aims, in oversight of students, in curriculum design, in standards of teaching and academic achievements and in its links with the local community. What they all have in common is effective leadership. … Without exception, the most important single factor in the success of these schools is the quality of leadership of the head."[1] The graph opposite shows the current distribution of school inspection results according to quality of leadership and management and overall achievement. Student achievement exceeds the quality of school leadership and management in less than 1% of schools.

School leadership is important because it creates, or fails to create, an environment in which students and teachers perform to the best

Figure 10: Percentage of schools with different ratings for school leadership and overall achievement (England)

% of all schools in each category

		Quality of leadership and management							
		Outstanding	Good	Satisfactory	Inadequate	Outstanding	Good	Satisfactory	Inadequate
Student achievement	Outstanding	12.3				15.5	0.8		
	Good	2.3	46.8	0.5		6.1	35.4	0.6	0.2
	Satisfactory		4.6	29.0	0.3		9.3	23.7	0.1
	Inadequate			2.1	2.0		0.1	4.8	3.3
		Primary (total = 100%)				Secondary (total = 100%)			

Source: Ofsted Inspection Judgments Autumn 2007 and Spring 2008

of their abilities. Good school leaders establish a culture of high expectations and shared responsibility for achieving them, create structures and devices that support teachers and students to teach and learn to the best of their ability, use resources effectively, and develop evidence-based strategies for improvement. They help teachers develop plans for improving teaching and learning and hold them accountable for implementing them. In the best schools, school leadership is distributed,[2] meaning that many different teachers play a role in the leadership of their school, and it is the sum of their efforts, rather than the actions of an individual principal, which provide the strong leadership described here. One seminal study of high-performing organizations in the business sector observed that one of their defining features was their "unusual ... ability to achieve extraordinary results through ordinary people."[3] The same could be said of high-performing schools.

Conversely, less effective schools and school leaders share an opposing set of features: they have variable expectations for how people should perform and behave, a lack of accountability, poor planning, inconsistent development of staff, and inefficient use of time and resources. That environment can have an equally negative impact on school performance; it is not just that good leadership makes teachers perform better; bad leadership makes them perform worse.[4]

These findings appear to hold across a wide range of school sys-

Figure 11: Characteristics of effective and less effective schools

Highly Effective Schools	Other Schools
• Focus on preparing students for college and careers	• Focus on preparing students for exams and graduation
• Consistently high expectations	• Variable expectations
• Embrace external standards and assessments	• Tolerate external standards and assessments
• Principals and teachers take responsibility for achievement	• Principals and teachers blame others for failure
• Assessment is used to plan and prepare for the future	• Assessment is used to measure past performance
• Teacher assignments and curriculum are based on needs of students	• Teacher assignments and curriculum are based on desires of teachers
• Support for new teachers is focused on instruction	• Support for new teachers is focused on social integration
• Instruction time is protected and used efficiently	• Instruction time is lost or wasted due to other pressures

Source: The Education Trust, *Gaining Traction Gaining Ground*, 2005

tems.[5] In Middle Eastern and African school systems, where principals generally have much less autonomy and control over their schools than in developed countries, excellent leadership is still consistently the defining feature of high-performing schools.[6] In the United States, quantitative studies of the factors affecting school performance confirm that the quality of school leadership has a substantial bearing on student achievement. One major review of the evidence concluded that "school leadership is second only to classroom teaching as an influence on pupil learning."[7] In fact, that conclusion understates the importance of school leadership because good leadership is not only important in and of itself, it is also the single most powerful way to improve classroom teaching.

Determining what makes a school leader effective and what policies work to increase the number of good leaders is not straight forward. The fact that their effects on student achievement are almost always indirect sometimes makes it difficult to measure how effective individual leaders are. Excellent school leaders demonstrate a wide range of leadership styles and practices, with differences often outweighing similarities, making it hard to identify common themes. Moreover, good school leaders may be effective in some situations but not in others. Principals who have been highly successful in getting good schools to perform better often struggle when challenged with turning around a poorly performing school.[8] Finally, the effectiveness of many school leaders varies over time, with some becoming more effective with experience while others become less effective as time goes by.

However, there is now a growing body of evidence on what makes an effective leader, and how to go about improving school leadership across the system. A few countries prove that that knowledge can be used to effect real change in standards of school leadership. England began a substantial program of investment in school leadership during the late 1990s. The program consisted of improved training, coaching and support for school leaders, new interventions to support schools where leadership and management were weak, new systems for evaluating and performance managing schools and school leaders, and continuous research into what was working and why. It was led by a new government body, the National College of School Leadership, to ensure that there was consistent focus on delivering results. The program produced significant improvement. The number of school leaders rated 'good', 'very good' or 'excellent' rose from one half to four fifths.[9] The time taken to turnaround failing schools fell from 38 months to 18 months over a seven-year period. The current generation of principals is the best trained in history. Though there is still room for much more improvement, the experience of both the English system and others shows that improving school leadership is challenging but achievable. Overall, they suggest that four broad approaches together lead to real improvement in standards of leadership and management:

- apprenticing and developing school leaders;
- attracting and selecting the right people for school leadership positions;
- empowering leaders and protecting their time; and
- intervening to address school failure.

Apprenticing and developing school leaders

Studies of effective school leaders show that, despite their apparent heterogeneity, they "almost all ... draw on the same repertoire of basic leadership practices."[10] More specifically, they tend to do four things well: establishing and communicating a vision for the school, understanding the people working in their schools and helping them to develop, organizing people within their schools so that they function well, and managing the program or teaching and learning. Ensuring that principals develop the skills and practices to do those things well lies at the core of ensuring that they are effective once in position.

In many school systems, principals receive little or no formal training before taking up their positions. One study of new principals in Europe found that "65% had received no formal or structured preparation for the job."[11] In other school systems, though training programs are offered or required, they do little to build the skills which new principals need to be effective in their roles. In the United States, for instance, most states require new principals to undertake a training program before they can apply for a position as a principal. In practice, "most principal training programs are designed to comply with certification statutes and regulations, and focus incorrectly on classroom-based educational theory rather than the practical skill development that working principals need."[12] 43 out of 50 states require principals to hold a master's degree, even though there is no evidence that this contributes to their effectiveness, and little reason to believe that advanced academic study would be a good preparation for the day-to-day work of school leadership and management. In a quarter of those states, the master's degree does not even have to be in a subject related to either education or leadership.[13] So a talented teacher who has successfully turned around a large department within their school is ineligible to become principal, while an ineffective teacher and leader with a master's degree in philosophy is. Other compulsory training requirements include a course on the state constitution in Arizona and an Alaskan Studies course for aspiring principals in America's northernmost State.[14]

In contrast, school systems which have succeeded in producing consistently good school leaders use a combination of formal training, apprenticeship, mentoring, and networking of principals to help new and aspiring school leaders to develop the practical skills they need to do their job well. In Singapore teachers with leadership potential are identified early in their career and promoted quickly to junior leadership positions in their schools. Before promotion to head of department within a school they attend a four-month course to prepare them to coach and mentor other school staff. However, the main period of apprenticeship as school leaders begins when they are selected as deputy principals, a role seen explicitly as a period of preparation for becoming a principal. Deputy principals are carefully paired with the serving principals who are best able to support their development, given individualized development plans, and rotated between schools once every two years to expose them to a wide range of leadership styles and school contexts. The final phase of training consists of a six-month full-time leadership program modelled on the executive MBA to boost their skills in creativity and strategic thinking. During the program, candidates undertake project work in schools where they design and lead improvement projects. The program includes a two-week internship at one of a range of multinational corporations where they shadow senior management to gain insight into top leadership in the private sector. The combination of strong apprenticeship of leaders in schools and high-quality formal training has enabled Singapore to establish a cadre of principals who are among the best in the world.

The same approach has proved effective elsewhere. KIPP uses a one-year program including apprenticeship in schools with high-performing principals and course material jointly developed by the Stanford schools of business and education to create a pipeline of new principals to run its schools. Similar programs have been developed by other school systems, including Boston, New York, and New Leaders for New Schools, an innovative program which selects and trains principals in Chicago, New York, San Francisco, Washington D.C., Baltimore, Memphis, Milwaukee, New Orleans, and Prince George's County. All have been successful in producing principals who, judged by the improvement trajectories of their schools, are more effective that principals trained on conventional programs.

Attracting and selecting the right people for leadership positions

However, good training and apprenticeship of new leaders are not enough without also ensuring that the right people are selected to become school leaders. While the research evidence shows that successful school leaders draw on a common set of practices, which can be developed through good training, it also shows that "a small handful of personal traits explain a high proportion of the variation in leadership effectiveness,"[15] or in other words, good school leaders are good primarily because of who they are, not what they do or how they have been trained. While most of the critical skills required of a principal can be acquired by anyone with the right support and motivation, "some [people] develop those capacities much more readily than others and some to a much higher level."[16] In particular, the most effective school leaders share a common set of intrinsic characteristics. They tend to be good problem solvers.[17] They are "open-minded and ready to learn from others, [...] flexible rather than dogmatic in their thinking within a system of core values, persistent (e.g. in pursuit of high expectations of staff motivation, commitment, learning, and achievement for all), resilient and optimistic."[18] The implication for school systems is that they need to be careful about selecting the right people to become school leaders, and determined in removing those who prove ineffective once in position.

Few school systems do either of those. In South Korea, candidates are eligible for appointment as principals primarily on the basis of age without any rigorous consideration of leadership or management ability. In Spain, selection criteria include years of teaching experience, date of application to become a principal, previous school posting, academic qualifications, and quality of work planning, but no criteria related to leadership or management ability. In other systems, though management and leadership abilities are given a prominent position in selection criteria, there are no rigorous processes for testing those abilities.[19] Even where good selection processes are in place, they may be executed poorly, compromising their effectiveness. This is particularly true in decentralized systems where the school boards charged with selecting new principals often lack experience of making selection decisions, a knowledge of what types of people will be effective school leaders, and an understanding of how to identify them. In England, where principals are selected by individual school boards, one review noted that "the recruitment process is sometimes characterised by variable rigour, the application of instinct and 'gut feel', a lack of foresight to future needs, a lack of knowledge about statutory requirements and standards, and a rush to advertise spurred by fear of delays in appointment."[20] New Zealand, where individual schools have their own elected school boards which are responsible for appointing the principal, has had similar problems, particularly in low-income areas where schools often struggle to find people with the right skills and expertise to serve on school boards.[21]

The problem is often compounded by a lack of good candidates for principal positions. In many countries vacancy rates for principals are increasing and relatively small numbers of senior school staff express a desire to take on the role of principal.[22] The lack of candidates reduces the potential for the system to be selective about who becomes a principal and encourages it to relax eligibility criteria and reduce expectations of school leaders. That can in turn lead to a further fall in the number of applicants if the status of the position falls because it is no longer perceived to be competitive. However, despite those challenges, a number of school systems demonstrate both that the supply of potential school leaders can be increased, and that those candidates with the highest potential to become excellent leaders can be identified. To achieve that, they do several things.

First, they develop good selection criteria and processes. Singapore evaluates deputy principals throughout their careers and training to become principal, and uses all of that information to make judgements about who will be an effective school leader and who will not. Career records and evaluations are complemented by situational testing during the final stages of the process, where actors play out difficult situations and candidates are assessed based on how they respond. Effective processes for screening potential leaders have also been developed in the United States by KIPP, New Leaders for New Schools, and some school districts, all of which focus on track records in leadership positions and demonstrated management skills. In school systems where control over principal appointments is devolved to local boards, more effective selection processes can be introduced by requiring principals to have a centrally-administered qualification, and then incorporating selection criteria into the award of that qualification which screen out unsuitable candidates.

In combination, school systems trying to improve the supply of good candidates have removed barriers that unnecessarily constrain the number of potential applicants. Several countries have schemes to help young teachers to become principals early in their careers if they show strong leadership potential. In England, teachers beginning their career who aspire to leadership positions can join a program called Future Leaders which provides leadership opportunities, coaching, mentoring, support, and the opportunity to become a principal within four years. They also remove training requirements which do not promote quality but do prevent good candidates from applying – for instance requiring that candidates have master's degrees or that they complete long theoretical courses on leadership and management.

More controversially, a few countries have experimented with allowing candidates from outside teaching to apply for school leadership positions. Almost all developed countries recruit principals exclusively from their teaching workforce.[23] There is a compelling logic for believing that somebody with experience of working within a school is likely to make a better school leader than somebody without that experience. This is particularly true in small schools, where the role of a principal is likely to be focused mainly on planning teaching and learning, developing staff, and the day-to-day running of the school, all of which require teaching experience and pedagogical knowledge. There are also good reasons for believing that it should be possible to recruit enough school leaders from within the teaching workforce; one policymaker notes that "if a country cannot recruit sufficient quality leaders from within its own teaching workforce, then it needs to worry about finding better teachers, not finding better principals."[24]

Nonetheless, there is good evidence from a number of countries that principals without experience in education can be highly effective school leaders.[25] This has particularly been true in larger schools. The larger the school, the less the principal is likely to be concerned with planning teaching and developing teachers, and the more the role becomes one of building and sustaining an organization. Other programs allow managers from outside education to becomes principals after one or two years of teaching experience. Both types of course can help to expand the pool of potential applicants.

In addition to developing good selection processes and removing barriers to applications, school, systems can increase the number of applicants by providing good training and mentoring for aspiring school leaders. Internationally, the most common reason that teachers do not apply for leadership positions in schools is that they feel that they lack the skills and preparation necessary to do the job well. Effective training and allowing individuals to take on progressively more responsibility as their development progresses helps to increase the pool of potential applicants by removing that obstacle. British research shows that "individuals who have gained some experience in leadership or aspects of it are more likely to be interested in leadership and to be confident in their capacity to do it."[26]

The overall ability of a school system to attract sufficient leadership talent depends critically on one other variable: the size of its schools. In England for instance, despite ten years of well executed reforms to improve the skills and supply of school leaders, government inspectors still find that around one third of schools do not have good leadership and management. One of the main reasons for that is the way in which the school system is structured. Schools in England operate, for the most part, as independent organizations. There is very little leadership or management at the school level which comes from outside the school itself. It also has relatively small schools, with an average of less than 400 students in each school. As a consequence, it needs to find 25,000 principals capable of independently leading and managing their schools. Singapore by contrast, has a more centralized model, with principals given far more support from the Ministry than in England. It also has much larger schools, with an average of 1,500 students per school. As a result, it needs fewer school leaders, and can leverage them more effectively. Singapore needs to find (and compensate) one effective principal from every 54 teachers it employs; England has just 18 to choose from.

One of the more popular interventions aimed at improving schools over the last decade, particularly in the United States, has been breaking up large schools into smaller independent schools. In the United States, the Gates Foundation has spent millions of dollars supporting plans to break up large schools. There are a few reasons why small schools might be expected to perform better than larger schools: it is easier to build a community among a group where students and teachers know each other, behaviour is often easier to manage, and there is stronger accountability among the staff for performance. In the words of the Gates Foundation's former head of education, "students in small schools are motivated, have higher attendance rates, and graduate and attend college in higher rates. Studies generally link improved outcomes in small schools to the rigor of instruction in small schools and to the quality of the relationships that exists among adults and students in small schools."[27]

In practice, most studies find little correlation between school size and achievement. On international tests of student achievement, large schools actually perform better than their smaller counterparts.[28] In England, the Netherlands and New Zealand, in particular, large schools outperform smaller schools by a significant margin, though this is partly caused by the fact that market mechanisms mean that good schools attract more students allowing them to expand. In most cases where large schools have been broken up into smaller schools, there has either been little corresponding improvement in performance, or that improvement has been attributed to other factors.[29] Perhaps unsurprisingly, taking the same students, the same teachers, the same curriculum and the same expectations out of a large school and placing them into several smaller schools does not tend to produce much change in teaching and learning. In the worst cases, reorganization of a large school into smaller schools has precipitated a total failure of the school, often because it was not possible to find enough good principals for the smaller schools.[30]

More importantly, there are other strategies for managing large schools which help to overcome the complexities caused by their size, while retaining the advantages of improved leadership and economies of scale. One promising approach has been to divide larger schools into 'learning clusters.' A school with 800 students and 40 teachers might be divided into four clusters of 200 students and 10 teachers, who then work together for most of the school day. The clusters capture the advantages of a smaller learning community while at the same time retaining the benefits of being part of a larger organization. A recent federal research study in the United States demonstrated that a range of different approaches to creating stronger learning communities in schools, including both structural changes to the organization of the schools and strategies for managing learning within those schools, could achieve similar effects to those sought through the creation of small schools.[31]

An alternative approach is to have smaller schools, but to strengthen the ties between them, for instance by arranging them into clusters with 'executive principals' managing several schools. "By sharing a high quality head, schools benefit from sharing that expertise and leadership. The money saved by not employing two heads can be ploughed into additional teaching support. … Usually this arrangement means that the head has more non-teaching time than the individual previous headship posts had, which means that they are better able to do the job and to provide leadership and support to the other staff. It also means that management points can be built in to provide one or more of the other teachers with some career progression – something currently lacking in many small schools."[32]

Empowering school leaders and protecting their time

Selecting the right people to become school leaders and developing them well builds the capacity to ensure that every school has effective leadership. However, unless those leaders are empowered to improve teaching and learning in their schools they are unlikely to become a powerful force for improvement. That does not necessarily mean devolving every aspect of school management down to the school level; as chapter six argues, there are strong reasons why it may often be best for the centre to retain control over some important policies and processes. However, principals who lack the power to make basic changes in their schools are unlikely to have much impact on the performance of those schools. In South Africa, Los Angeles, and several other large school systems, principals are not allowed to enter a teacher's classroom while they are teaching without written permission from the teacher obtained weeks in advance.[33] In Germany, many government schools have almost no control over their budgets.[34] Both constraints prevent school leaders from leading improvement in instruction. In some school systems where principals have very little control over their own schools, the best schools are often those which are run by principals who break the rules; in the words of the principal of one high-performing school in the Middle East: "Of course, we never asked the Ministry for permission to do these things; they would take years to approve it, and even then they would say no to a good idea."

In those and other school systems, school leaders generally tend to be seen primarily as managers of school administration rather than as leaders of improvement. Principals in France say that they spend just four hours each week managing the curriculum and teaching staff, compared to 18 hours each week on those activities in Singapore and New Zealand. Not only does that focus on administration create a deficit of educational leadership, it also means that good teachers are less likely to apply to become school leaders in the first place, because school leadership is seen as a way of escaping the classroom, rather than as a way to help other teachers and students succeed; in the words of one Eastern European expert, "in our system, those who can, do; those who can't, teach; and those who can't teach lead the schools."[35]

Both the amount of time principals spend at work and what they do during that time are correlated with the results their schools achieve. The more time principals in a school system spend working in their schools, the higher the achievement of their students.[36] The PISA data shows that what principals do – and in particular, the extent to which they monitor lessons and evaluate teacher performance – has a significant effect on how well their schools perform.[37]

Successful school systems do a number of things to ensure that principals are leaders of teaching rather than leaders of administration. First, they set clear expectations for how principals will spend their time. In Edmonton, principals were asked to spend half of the school day working with teachers in classrooms.[38] In Boston, schools leaders are expected to be "in classrooms every day, talking with students about what they are learning and conferring with teachers about their informal observations and decisions on next steps."[39]

Second, they ensure that evaluation and incentives for principals are based mainly on how well they lead teaching and improvement in their schools, rather than the quality of administration in their schools. In some European and Middle Eastern school systems evaluation and monitoring of school leaders are focused entirely on the extent to which they operate their schools well, with predictable effects on how they spend their time. Conversely, in Singapore, the quality of administration and school operation contributes just 6% to a principal's overall evaluation score.[40]

Finally, they reduce the administrative load on school leaders to free up their time for other activities. For instance, Boston invested in improved technology to automate much of the administration which used to take place in schools and release principal time. England uses regular consultations with principals to reduce reporting and bureaucratic requirements to a minimum, and is currently piloting programs to provide schools with dedicated administrators who would undertake what remains.

Intervening to address school failure

Improving the selection, development, and empowerment of school leaders lies at the core of ensuring that every school has effective leadership. However, even in the best school systems, school leaders can become less effective over time or be confronted with challenges which overwhelm the school's own capacity to improve. In school systems which have not historically selected and developed school leaders well, failures of school leadership may be more common. The final component of ensuring that every school has effective leadership is having robust mechanisms for dealing with failures of school leadership and management.

New College School in Leicester serves one of the most deprived areas in the United Kingdom. It was formed in 1999 through the merger of three failing schools against the wishes of the local community. The resulting school had more than 1,600 students, a sprawling set of disconnected buildings, and academic performance well below national averages.

Despite those challenges, the school performed well for the first few years. An evaluation by the government's school inspectors in 2002 concluded that it was a broadly effective with "a significant amount of very good teaching … very strong clear leadership … [and] high levels of commitment amongst staff."[41] However, by the following year, the school had entered a swift decline. Standards of behaviour had become extremely low, with students shouting, swearing, and fighting between classes, and lessons disrupted by constant interruptions, chatting, and petty misbehaving. More than 350 students were suspended during a single year, and one in five failed to attend school each day. Staff morale and expectations plummeted, as did students' expectations of themselves. One quarter of the teaching still remained good. In those classes teachers controlled behaviour well, delivered lessons which were appropriate and interesting, and students made progress. However, the vast majority of teaching was ineffective. Curriculum content was uninteresting and often too hard for students to understand. Poor teaching would lead to boredom, lower expectations, and misbehaviour, which slowed the pace of the lessons until they ground to a halt. School leaders were unable to address the school's diverse and complex set of problems, and attempts to improve conditions in the school were unsuccessful. Many teachers had come to accept that failure was inevitable, and that low standards were a necessary consequence of the area in which the school was located and the students and communities it served.

In December 2003 the school was inspected by Ofsted and

placed into Special Measures. The Special Measures category designates schools which have both poor levels of teaching and learning and a low probability of improvement without external support and intervention. Schools in Special Measures have to develop and implement improvement plans, and receive extra funding, external support, and more frequent monitoring until they improve.

After it was placed in Special Measures, New College drifted for a further two years. School leaders failed to get a hold on the problems the school faced or come up with effective solutions to them. As low standards persisted, many parents took their children out of the school, with total enrolment falling by half. Standards ultimately fell to the point where the school officially became the lowest performing school in England. Staff began to see the school's problems as intractable, with morale and expectations falling even further.

Yet, subsequent events proved that New College's failure was neither as intractable or as irreversible as it seemed. In January 2006 a new principal and board were appointed to lead a turnaround of the school, bringing with them a number of managers from other schools. They quickly stabilized the school, brought behaviour under control, set out a vision and strategy for improvement, and reversed the culture of low expectations. Within two months, the school had been removed from the Special Measures category. The number of students achieving good results aged 15 jumped from 10% to 27% in a single year. By the middle of 2007, inspectors concluded that "the College is a calm and orderly community that provides good care, guidance and support for its students. … There has been dramatic improvement in students' behaviour, attitudes, punctuality and attendance. … The college's rapid transformation has been the result of excellent senior leadership, rigorous self-evaluation, the hard work of staff and their willingness to embrace changes. … Many of the improvements have been realised by new appointments, but much has also been achieved by the existing staff. Teachers who were beleaguered and whose morale was low have been given new confidence and the motivation to work hard. ... Students say that the college is unrecognisable compared to how it was a year ago."[42]

New College's turnaround demonstrates that schools which have run into severe difficulties can be improved, often mainly through the efforts of existing staff and even when the school faces strong external pressures and challenges. In New College's case recovery was swift, though it was a long time before decisive action was taken. The best school systems prove that failure is not a necessary feature of a school system; Finland and Singapore no longer have failing schools. Others prove that it can be massively reduced; England halved the number of failing schools in its school system between 1998 and 2005 through a combination of better monitoring, evidence-based strategies for improvement, and zero-tolerance of schools which were not improving.[43] Around 10% of failing schools which did not demonstrate improvement were closed, with students either transferred to other local schools, or a new school opened on the same site with new leadership, a new name, new staff, and often new facilities. In a few cases, failing schools merged with nearby schools with higher performance to create a federation which provided stronger leadership, management and access to models of good teaching for the weaker school. Though it has yet to find ways to pre-empt and prevent school failure in a devolved system, England's experience shows that failure can be detected and tackled quickly, and that doing so can raise standards of leadership in the system as a whole.

The quality of school leadership and management is one of the most important factors affecting student achievement and learning. Moreover, in the absence of good leadership, school systems will struggle to implement many of the other reforms that might improve performance in schools, because good leadership is often necessary to enable schools to implement those reforms. For instance, setting standards, strengthening inspections and assessments, introducing competition between schools, or increasing accountability for performance are all unlikely to lead to improvement in the absence of good leadership. However, once schools have good leadership, those actions can all have a substantial impact on performance. The next chapter examines the impact of standards, inspections, and assessments, while the following chapter looks at structuring the system to improve performance.

5.

Challenge, flow, and the power of expectations

(Setting standards and measuring whether they are achieved)

Setting high expectations for performance and measuring whether or not they are achieved can help to drive improvements in teaching and learning. Assessments and school reviews can raise expectations, provide information to inform improvement, and form the basis for a range of other policies to improve the performance of schools. However they can also be damaging and controversial when focused too narrowly, implemented badly, or linked to teacher compensation. Moreover, in the absence of capacity to improve in schools, they are unlikely to have much positive effect. The best school systems combine high standards and accountability with strong support for improvement and determined professionalism to achieve consistently high performance.

Challenge and flow

Mihaly Csikszentmihalyi was born in 1934 in the Italian seaport of Fiume where his father was the Hungarian consul.[1] He grew up in Mussolini's Italy, attending schools in Rome, Florence, and Fiume, and spending part of the Second World War in an Italian prison camp. After the War his father was promoted and became the Hungarian ambassador to Italy. However, the posting proved to be short-lived. By 1948, the communist takeover of Hungary was complete and Mihaly's father, who refused to return to Hungary, was replaced as ambassador and subsequently sentenced to death in absentia by the new government in Budapest. Mihaly, meanwhile, become fascinated by psychology. He learned English, his fourth language, and at the age of 22 travelled to the United States to study at the University of Chicago. Struck that Americans living in a country with few of the troubles of post-war Europe seemed to be no more satisfied with their lives than the people he had left behind in Italy, he spent most of the next fifty years studying the mother of all questions: what makes people happy?

In the course of his work he carried out a series of large field experiments. Participants in the experiments were asked to wear an electronic paging device or a programmed watch. At random points during the day, the device would beep, and the participants had to write down what they were doing at that moment, where they were, what they were thinking about, and how they felt. In total, Csikszentmihalyi and his colleagues in other universities around the world captured more than 250,000 moments in peoples' lives. He combined these with the data from thousands of interviews and case studies,[2] and developed a simple theory to explain how the things we do influence our emotions.[3]

The data showed that how a person feels at any one time is determined mainly by the combination of two things: how challenging they find the situation which they are in, and whether or not they feel that they have the skills necessary to meet that challenge. When people feel an average level of challenge and an average level of skill, their emotions are neutral. However, as those levels of skill and challenge change, a distinct and predictable set of emotions emerge. When people are in situations where they feel a high level of challenge, but a low level of skill, they become anxious. These are moments of stress, family problems, driving in difficult traffic, or taking on complex new tasks. At these moments people are alert but unhappy and often unproductive as a result. When people are in situations where they feel both a low level of challenge and a low level of skill, they feel apathetic. Low challenge and high skill, activities like reading or easy tasks at work, lead to relaxation. When people feel a high level of skill and a medium level of challenge, they feel control. However, the point at which people are happiest is when they feel a sense of 'flow'.

Flow was the term that Csikszentmihalyi used to describe the combination of high challenge and high skill. He used the word 'flow' because people so often used the analogy of being carried away by a flow of energy when describing the experience; it was the feeling of a runner competing in a marathon, a surgeon carrying out an operation, an artist creating a painting, a musician playing in a symphony, a farmer working the fields, a politician addressing a rally, or an excellent teacher teaching a tough topic. Consistently, these were the moments when people felt the happiest, the most alive, and the most fulfilled. It was also when their performance was at its best, their creativity greatest, and their productivity highest.

Good schools tend to be the ones which provide those same conditions for their students and teachers: high expectations for teaching and learning combined with the environment and support to develop the skills need to meet them.[4] The same is true of high-performing organizations in other sectors of the economy.[5] It is also true of school systems: the best school systems are those which provide both constructive challenge to students and schools along with the resources and support to succeed.

Most efforts to improve the quality of teaching in schools can be characterized either as efforts to provide more challenge to the system or as efforts to support improvements in skills. Like other organizations, school systems perform best when they achieve the right combination of the two. If a school reform only increases the level of the challenge in the system, for instance by introducing tougher exams or performance-based pay for teachers, the resulting improvement is likely to be limited, and the reform is likely to generate a lot of the negative emotions that Csikszentmihalyi discovered through his work: anxiety leading to frustration and anger (in a political context, this manifests itself as opposition from teacher unions or boycotts of tests). Reforms which only provide support to develop skills run similar risks of ineffectiveness: without challenge, investment in skills can be wasted and there may be little incentive for schools or teachers to make the difficult changes required to develop their staff or themselves. Successful school systems and school reforms are characterized by the combination of the two.

There are many ways to create the right level of challenge in a school system. Often the most effective is to recruit teachers who set high expectations for themselves and are driven by a strong personal motivation to help every child succeed. Another is to ensure that all schools are led by excellent principals who set challenging but achievable expectations for themselves, their schools, their students, and

Figure 12: Challenge and support in school reform

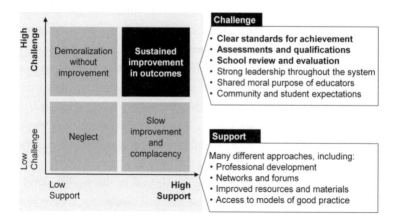

Source: Adapted from Barber, M., *Delivering Results: The Theory and Practice of Whole System Reform*, 2006

their teachers. Changing the organizational structure of the school system – strengthening accountability, unleashing market forces, giving parents the right to choose which school their children attend, or opening up the school market to new providers – can sometimes provide constructive challenge to the system. However, the most direct way of increasing the level of challenge in a school system is to set standards and then measure whether or not they are being achieved though assessments and school reviews.

Assessment and school reviews allow the system to set expectations for performance and measure whether they are achieved

The insight that examinations can be a powerful driver of improvement is not a new one. The first national examination system was established in China under the Sui Dynasty in 605 and persisted through to the early part of the twentieth century. The Imperial Examination System was notoriously brutal: examinations, which tested military strategy, government, economics, law, geography, and Chinese literature, could last for up to three days, during which time candidates were locked in cubicles together with a desk and a bed to complete the paper. Though originally intended as a mechanism for improving the selection of civil servants rather than as a means of reforming the education system, the examinations drove the system of teaching and learning across China for the length of their existence. Modern examiners note that little has changed about the power of examinations over students and schools since then: what gets tested is what gets learned, and how it is tested determines how it gets learned.

Most developed countries, and about half of the world's developing countries, have some form of national assessment system.[6] In about two-thirds of the developed world, graduation from school depends on successful completion of an externally-set examination. In other systems, tests may be 'low-stakes'; without any consequences for schools or individual students who fail to meet the standard. Over the past two decades, there has been an increase in the use of external assessments in school systems, most notably in the United States under the No Child Left Behind legislation. Under the Act, first passed in January 2002, every state is required to set standards for proficiency in reading and mathematics at different grade levels, measure student performance against those standards every year, and achieve regular improvement in the results. The results of the assessments have to be published not only for a state as a whole, but also for different minority and student groups, and for individual schools.

An alternative way of measuring school performance is through school reviews or inspections. In a number of school systems, including New Zealand, the Netherlands, England, and Hong Kong, all schools are reviewed by independent teams of inspectors on a regular basis, on average once every three years. The teams evaluate the performance of a school and the achievement of its students over the course a number of days through observation of teaching and learning, interviews, surveys, and analysis of relevant data. At the end of the review, they produce a report outlining strengths, areas for development, and how the school compares to other schools on a range of review criteria. The reviews are based on detailed standards covering different aspects of school performance: student achievement, spiritual, social and cultural development, the quality of curriculum and teaching, the quality of pastoral care, the effectiveness of leadership and management, and the strength of the school's relationships with parents and the community. They aim both to provide an assessment of the performance of the school across a wide set of criteria, and to identify reasons for underperformance where it exists.

Both assessment and review are associated with higher performance in schools

There is strong evidence that both assessment and review, when implemented well, lead to improved performance in schools. Before the No Child Left Behind legislation made state assessments mandatory, American states which already had external assessments were improving twice as fast as those without. These gains were evident even when all other policies and inputs were held constant,[7] and the improvement was significant, equivalent to 10% additional progress each year. Since the No Child Left Behind Act was passed, schools in the United States have achieved the biggest national improvement in numeracy and literacy since records began.

Across the developed world as whole, school systems with system-wide standards and assessment perform better than those without.[8] Again, the difference is significant, with OECD countries with external standards-based examinations scoring 21 points higher on the PISA tests than those without standards-based exams; equivalent to more than half a year of schooling. A study of Mexican states showed that those which had a system of standards and assessment performed better than those without, and that those states which made the results public and used them to design policies, strategies and interventions, performed even better. These differences were large; equivalent to taking the lowest-performing state to the average level, or an average state to the top-performing spot.[9]

There is similar evidence demonstrating that school reviews also have a positive impact on performance, although that impact is more variable and depends crucially on the capacity of schools to react to recommendations or weaknesses. Since the regular inspection system was introduced in England, there has been a steady reduction in the number of failing schools, the time taken to turnaround failing schools, and the number of lessons judged to be unsatisfactory, all of which have been linked to the inspection process.[10] Cross-country comparisons of African school systems have found that school inspections have a positive effect on student achievement, although the extent of the benefit depends on how the inspections are implemented.[11] Despite a widely held belief to the contrary, an overwhelming majority of principals in countries with balanced school review systems say that the reviews contribute to improving the performance of schools.

However, reviews and assessments can, as is discussed later, also be both controversial and damaging if they are implemented badly, or if the results are used for the wrong purposes. Moreover, it is important to recognize that standards, testing, inspection, and account-

Figure 13: The impact of external standards-based assessments

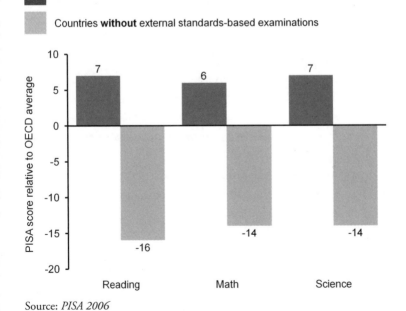

■ Countries **with** external standards-based examinations

■ Countries **without** external standards-based examinations

Source: *PISA 2006*

ability do not, in and of themselves, do anything to improve the quality of teaching and learning in schools. As John Dunford, leader of one of the main teaching unions in England says, "weighing the pig does not fatten it." Improvement depends on teachers and schools accepting the standards and changing what they do as a result of the information, insights and challenge that come from the system. Where the capacity, resources, support, autonomies, or motivation to make those changes are absent, improvement is unlikely to occur.

In the majority of cases though, assessments and school reviews have led to improvements in school performance. That improvement occurs for three main reasons: because they can help to raise expectations for performance across the system; because they provide information to students, teachers, schools, and the system as a whole on both strengths and weaknesses; and finally because they form the basis for a range of other policies which lead to improvement in schools.

Assessments and reviews help to raise expectations

In any organization, the vision and expectations set by leadership are a powerful driver of performance. In the case of schools, expectations seem to be particularly important. One study found that when teachers had higher expectations of their students, "that alone was enough to cause an increase of 25 points in students' IQ scores,"[12] and high expectations are a consistent characteristic of both the best teachers and the best schools.[13] Setting robust standards for student and school performance across the system can in and of itself help to clarify and raise the expectations of teachers, schools, students, and parents. Those standards are often even more powerful when combined with assessments or school reviews. Tom Birmingham, one of the architects of the state tests and standards in Massachusetts recalls that "some districts didn't take standards seriously till we came out with the test. ... Then we saw a sea change. There was a renewed focus, particularly with kids who posed the biggest challenges."[14]

One way to demonstrate the effect of standards on the performance of schools is to compare achievement in the different states in the United States. Although the No Child Left Behind Act requires every state to develop a system of standards and assessment, it is up to each state to decide how to implement those provisions. In particular, individual states set their own standards for achievement, determine what they will consider to be 'proficient' performance, and decide what they will consider to be adequate yearly progress for both the system as a whole and for individual schools.

Perhaps unsurprisingly, there is a wide variation in what states decided the target level of proficiency should be. Some states set high standards for what they considered to be proficient performance in reading and mathematics. Massachusetts, for instance, already had in place its MCAS testing system, with one of the toughest definitions of proficiency in the United States. Other states considered a much more basic level of achievement to be proficient. The following graph shows some of the different state standards for proficiency in mathematics at grades 4 and 8 converted into equivalent scores on the national NAEP mathematics test.[15] On average, students progress about 10 points on the NAEP scale for every year they spend at school, which means that the difference between the grade eight standard for proficiency in Tennessee, and the same standard in Montana, is equivalent to more than eight years of schooling. In Tennessee, North Carolina, and West Virginia, the grade eight tests are easier than the grade four test in Massachusetts.

This variation in standards has a noticeable effect on how much progress students make at school. In the states with high expectations for student achievement, students make more progress between the end of grade four and the end of grade eight than in the states with lower expectations. This effect is not very strong: many other factors affect how much students learn, and good teaching and learning often take place in states which set low expectations for achievement. It also gets weaker the higher expectations are raised. Once the progress expected of each student is already significantly above what they are actually likely to achieve, making the standards tougher has no further impact on performance. Nonetheless, there is a significant effect, and student in states with high expectations make roughly 10% more progress than those in states with low expectations.[16]

The impact of high expectations is further amplified when the

Figure 14: Comparing state definitions of proficiency in Mathematics at grades 4 and 8 in the United States

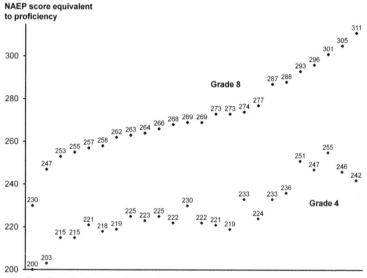

Source: National Center for Education Statistics, *Mapping 2005 State Proficiency Standards onto the NAEP Scales*, 2007

assessments used to test them form the basis of a system of qualifications. Well-designed qualifications, including graduation certificates, are highly valuable to students because they allow them to demonstrate achievement to future employers or institutes of further education. In England, holders of school-leaving qualifications in Mathematics (particularly A-Levels in mathematics) will earn substantially more than other school leavers, even if they do not go to university. Because of that value, the assessments used as the basis of those qualifications have a powerful influence on what gets taught and what gets learned. Conversely, when there are no standards for graduation from school, or when standards are too low, that can reduce the incentive for teachers and students to tackle difficult material. In Massachusetts linking the MCAS assessments to graduation had a powerful effect on schools and students: "[Before that] a Massachusetts diploma meant nothing. We only required English, U.S. history, and four years of gym, which is a testimony to the strength of the gym teachers' lobby. ... Making MCAS a graduation requirement was essential to motivate students to try harder."[17]

Similar effects on performance when school systems set high standards for schools are apparent but harder to prove. Boston's *Six Essentials For Whole School Improvement* sets out a powerful vision for Boston's schools in six key areas – instruction, professional development, student work and data, leadership, resources, and families and community – which has been used as the basis for most of the city's improvement efforts. Principals in Boston reported that the standards both raised the expectations of principals and schools of their own performance and acted as a reference point for measuring progress towards the vision. One review of the inspection system in England noted that "frameworks – which have consistently received very positive responses in consultations – can assist institutions in identifying what is broadly accepted as constituting good or effective practice."[18] One teachers' union in England described the first Ofsted inspection standards as "the best book on school management that has ever appeared from official sources. It is a well polished mirror in which to reflect – and reflect on – the performance and procedures of all areas of school life."[19] When the review system is used to highlight areas of strong practice, those examples can also themselves be powerful drivers of expectations in other schools, particularly when they prove what can be achieved in challenging circumstances.

Reviews and assessments contribute to improvement by providing objective information on performance

The second way in which assessment and review can help to improve student performance is by providing schools with an objective assessment of their own performance, and how that performance compares to the best schools in comparable circumstances. Good assessment systems provide detailed feedback on individual student achievement, adjusted for the background and prior attainment of students, which enables schools to plan teaching, identify weaknesses, and ensure that they have a realistic appraisal of how the performance of their students compares to the standards. There is good evidence that when school systems introduce assessments that also helps to improve teachers' own assessments of their students' performance. As Michael Fullan notes: "you can't achieve better results without establishing mechanisms for open data collection and use."[20]

School reviews are more useful than assessments in this respect, because they help schools to understand not only their overall performance but also the factors which contribute to that performance, and by extension, which areas need attention in order to improve. They also give a better indication of how a school will perform in the future. Whereas assessment is a lagging indicator which measures the results of past teaching and learning, schools reviews give a snapshot of present performance and capacity for the future. As a result, they can be more useful in predicting school failure and thereby assisting schools and the school system in taking action to prevent it. This is particularly important in weaker schools, which are unlikely to have a realistic assessment of their own performance.[21]

For the system as a whole, highlighting areas of success helps to recognize achievement and provides valuable examples of effective practice for the rest of the system. England and New Zealand now have some of the largest databases of school performance in the world, allowing them to quickly identify areas of excellent performance and then understand the practices and instruments which have produced it. This information is essential to informed efforts to improve; as Andreas Schleicher, the Director of the PISA program puts it: "In the darkness, all students, schools and education systems look the same. And when we know little about the strengths and weaknesses of schools and education systems, it is difficult to help them."[22] At a broader level, it also provides policymakers with the information they need to formulate better policies and address issues, and it provides the public and press with the information which they need to hold governments to account for the performance of the school system. In the best school systems, it can help shift the public debate on education from one based on impressions and anecdotes to one based on hard evidence about the performance of schools.

Assessment and review are the basis for a range of other policies to improve schools

Finally, assessment and review are an essential foundation for a range of other policies which can improve the performance of schools. For instance, they can be used to identify schools where additional support or intervention is required to prevent failure or drive improvement. School reviews are particularly useful in this respect because, unlike assessments, they provide an indication of whether or not a school has the capacity to improve on its own, and what types of external support it might need if not. When large-scale reforms are being implemented, reviews can quickly show whether the reform is working and which schools or types of school might need additional resources or support in order to ensure that changes are implemented successfully.

Reviews and assessment also form an essential foundation for any system of accountability or performance management for schools. Without a robust system for measuring performance in a way that is credible and trusted by schools, it is impossible to hold schools and their leaders to account for that performance. Similarly, they are also essential to making parental choice and competition between schools drivers of improvement. In the absence of publicly-available review or assessment data, parents normally find it difficult to assess the true performance of schools, which in turn makes it difficult for them to make informed choices about which schools will provide the best education for their children. Under those circumstances, choice and market mechanisms are unlikely to lead to real improvements in quality.

In many school systems, assessments and reviews have underpinned efforts to improve. When well designed they can become extremely popular with schools. For instance, though vocal opposition to the accountability arrangements in England remains, in reality, four times as many headteachers say that the benefits of inspection outweigh the negatives as say the opposite, and that proportion is rising over time.[23] However, review and assessment can be extremely controversial instruments for improving schools. More importantly, there are some cases where they have clear negative effects on individual schools and sometimes the system as a whole. Several problems in particular are common causes of assessments and reviews failing to have the impact they should.

Assessments and reviews can be damaging when they are focused too narrowly

The first problem is that when assessments and reviews are focused too narrowly they can, precisely because of their power over what happens in schools and classrooms, lead the system to focus on those things which are measured to the exclusion of other important aspects of schooling. They can also cause schools to engage in behaviours which improve scores or review results without producing any real educational benefit. This happened in the United States after the introduction of the No Child Left Behind Act, under which states were required to measure and publish school performance in mathematics and reading. There was an "immediate reaction [to the tests] in terms of focusing teaching on relevant subjects or even relevant students near performance cut-offs; of increased exclusions from tests; of explicit cheating on tests; and of like attempts to improve scores in ways other than improving student learning."[24] As many as two-thirds of districts reduced the amount of time allocated to other subjects in order to increase the amount of instruction in mathematics and reading.[25] When tests are linked to rewards or penalties for schools or teachers, these effects can be even more severe. In England between 1862 and 1895, the government operated a pay-for-performance system in which teachers were paid according to the performance of their students in tests of three, and later six, key subjects. Many teachers came to focus on those subjects to the exclusion of other important aspects of education which were not being measured. As an official government report at the time noted, "too many teachers narrow their sense of duty to the six standards, or what they sometimes call 'the paying subjects.'"[26]

In the case of basic skills such as numeracy and literacy, there may be some justification for focusing the attention of schools on ensuring that every child reaches a good standard of achievement. Levels of numeracy and literacy are the best predictors of future success in schooling and the labour market and constitute a foundation without which it is difficult to succeed in all other parts of schooling. They are also a prerequisite for almost all other aspects of education: without good skills in reading and logical thinking, students are unlikely to succeed in any other subject.[27]

Requiring schools to ensure that students pass tests in numeracy and literacy also has less of an effect on other areas of the curriculum than is commonly assumed. When student performance in reading rises, scores in other subjects tend to rise as well.[28] More generally, getting students to score well in numeracy and literacy requires schools to do a set of things – planning, investing in staff development, improving behaviour, and others – which are the foundation for success in all other areas of learning and development as well. In England, it is sometimes claimed that testing in core subjects has forced out other aspects of the curriculum and made schooling a stressful and difficult experience for children. The data actually shows that the reverse is true. 98% of English primary schools with good levels of student achievement also have good ratings for the spiritual, moral, social, and cultural development of their students, and 99.5% provide an enjoyable experience for their students.[29] Conversely, schools with lower levels of academic achievement generally have lower ratings in other areas as well, and their students are less likely to enjoy school. Studies in the United States have found similar correlations between scores in numeracy and literacy tests and almost all of the other outcomes which schools are expected to produce, even after controlling for the background of students in the schools.

Nonetheless, a narrowly focused assessment system will ultimately result in some distortion of priorities for students and schools. This problem is compounded when the assessments only test a narrow range of skills. In the Middle East, many school systems use tests which only assess students on how much information they have remembered and whether they can solve basic problems. Unsurprisingly, graduates from those school systems tend to know a lot of facts, but are not good at applying them and rarely master more complex skills such as making an extended argument or interpreting unfamiliar data. Similar problems can arise when the assessments use only a limited set of question types. Just under half of America's school students live in states where the tests used to meet the requirements of the No Child Left Behind Act include no open-ended questions, and typically a large proportion of multiple-choice questions.[30] These types of test can only measure a small subset of what students actually need to be able to do and understand in order to be proficient in mathematics and literacy, and are often written in ways which allow students to increase their scores by extensive practice of the question types or use of testing strategies, rather than by increasing their actual competency in the subjects tested. Though there is good evidence that the introduction of assessments has led to real improvements in student abilities across the United States as a whole,[31] in many states that improvement is inevitably less than it would be were the tests better aligned with the outcomes that the school system seeks to produce.

One advantage of school reviews in this context is that they can help to balance out the effect of a narrow assessment system. However good they may be, written tests can never capture all of the important outcomes that education seeks to produce. In contrast, well-designed reviews can evaluate student personal development, extracurricular provision, health, safety, happiness, and a range of other outcomes which cannot be measured though examinations. Other school systems, for instance Alberta in Canada, use surveys of students, teachers, and parents, combined with measures such as dropout and transition rates to balance out the assessment system. In doing so, they force schools to focus on a wider set of priorities than just ensuring that students pass standardized tests.

Reviews and assessments can cause controversy when implemented badly

The second set of problems arises when assessments or reviews are implemented badly. Both assessment and review are susceptible to small errors in implementation because for either to be useful, they not only have to be reliable measures of performance, but they also have to be perceived to be reliable. Relatively low levels of error can easily undermine the credibility and acceptance of an accountability system. When assessments are linked to qualifications, on which students' future earnings or careers may depend, the risk of small errors producing crises which bring down the credibility of the entire system is even greater.

In England, the effectiveness of the first inspection system was undermined by a lack of consistency in standards and poor work by inspectors. A purge of ineffective inspectors in 1903 exposed how far quality had fallen. Official evaluations of inspectors noted that one was "notorious as a fool ... inconceivably futile and worse than others" while another had "sunk into so deep a rut that he will never again see over the edge, nor is able to do anything definite either in this rut or in any other rut."[32] The best modern-day examination and inspection systems are controlled and managed to produce a high level of reliability. Teams of school inspectors in England, for instance, are evaluated by each other and the schools they inspect on every inspection, and computers cross-check inspection judgements for anomalies in the work of individual inspectors. Training and inspection processes have been standardized and refined to reduce errors in judgements. The satisfaction rate among headteachers with the inspection system is consistently around 90%, which far exceeds the satisfaction rate for other service organizations (banks, for instance, typically score around 60% to 70% in surveys of customer satisfaction).[33]

Minor design flaws in the system can also easily compromise their usefulness. For instance, when schools are given a long period of advance notice before their inspection that can compromise both the validity of the inspection regime and teaching and learning in the schools themselves. In England during the 1990s, schools were given several weeks advance notice of their inspection date, causing some to over-prepare to the extent that the preparation interfered with usual teaching and learning.[34] One inspector reported eating lunch with a group of children in a school after inspecting a lesson when one of the children asked, "did you like our lesson?" The inspector replied that he had, to which the child responded, "that's good because we've been practising it for three weeks."

Review and assessments must be independent of those responsible for improving the school system

A third set of problems arises when assessments and reviews are controlled by the same people who are responsible for improving schools. Under those circumstances, the objectivity of the reviews or assessments can be compromised either intentionally or unintentionally by the need to demonstrate improvement in the system. In England, the board of the original school inspectorate included representatives from the main bodies responsible for running the schools. The first school inspector, Seymour Tremenheere, was dismissed in 1842 after just three years in post when his study of educational provision in London concluded that there were only three efficient schools in the city, a finding which was undoubtedly true.[35] His dismissal and subsequent appointment as an Inspector of Mines can hardly have encouraged others to report the darker side of schooling in England with the same degree of candour. As recently as the early 1990s, when the new GCSE examinations were being introduced, grade inflation was actively encouraged to ensure that the new examinations were seen to be a success.[36]

Many school systems have combated those problems by making

assessment and review structurally independent of the organizations responsible for improving school performance. In New Zealand the Education Review Office, which is responsible for inspecting and reporting on the quality of teaching and learning in schools, is a completely independent organization with its own Ministerial portfolio.[37] In Singapore, examinations are run by a separate examinations authority, the Singapore Examinations and Assessment Board. Some school systems have gone further by using international partners to quality assure standards in their assessments. Both Singapore and Hong Kong, for instance, have long partnered with British assessment authorities to quality assure their examinations and ensure that standards remain constant over time.

Linking review and assessment to teacher compensation rarely leads to improvement

A final set of problems emerges when school systems try to link teacher compensation to the results of school reviews or assessments. The idea that paying teachers based on the progress which their students make can lead to improvement is popular and intuitively powerful. Linking compensation to performance would incentivize teachers to perform better and reward those who do. It would also penalize those who perform poorly or fail to improve, and perhaps encourage them to leave the system. As Bill Gates, who has donated more to improving American education than any other individual, points out, "it's astonishing to me to have a system that doesn't allow us to pay more for someone with scarce abilities, that doesn't allow us to pay more to reward strong performance. That is tantamount to saying teacher talent and performance don't matter and that's basically saying students don't matter."[38]

However, in practice, pay-for-performance has only been implemented in a handful of school systems,[39] and does not appear to be an effective way of raising performance, particularly, when the overall performance of the system is not already strong. One study noted that "there is no example of a troubled district that has successfully used merit pay to improve its performance."[40] There are three reasons why, despite its apparent promise, pay-for-performance does not lead to improvement in schools.

First, paying teachers based on performance seems to have little impact on what they actually do in the classroom. While setting standards and introducing assessments has a powerful effect on behaviour in the school system, the additional power of linking a portion of teacher compensation to those standards is small. In every single case where pay-for-performance schemes have been introduced, there has either been no significant change in classroom practice, or changes have been attributed to other initiatives that were implemented in parallel, for instance additional training.

The fact that pay-for-performance has little effect on performance or motivation is unsurprising. The value of financial incentives comes from the fact that they provide additional motivation for a workforce to improve its performance. They are most effective in cases where the workforce has the potential to perform better, but lacks motivation because the work they do is intrinsically unrewarding. Most teachers already draw a strong sense of motivation from the purpose which their work serves, and where that motivation has been broken, for instance by poor skills or poor leadership and management in schools, those barriers are unlikely to be overcome by small financial incentives. This is consistent with other professions where the main drive comes from a belief that the enterprise – in this case, preparing the next generation for the future – is worthwhile. In cases where pay-for-performance has been introduced for those professions, the results have generally been disappointing.[41]

Second, it is very difficult to implement a pay-for-performance system well. Introducing a pay-for-performance system depends on being able to accurately and reliably determine the performance level of each teacher. The issue of reliability is extremely important. When calculating a person's compensation, it is not acceptable to have a system which gets it right 80% of the time. To be fair and to gain the respect and approval of the teaching workforce, evaluation systems have to be extremely reliable. Opposition to evaluation schemes from teachers often arises from the lack of reliability inherent in many of the systems proposed.

Though simple in theory, reliably measuring the impact of individual teachers by testing their students is extremely difficult in practice. By the time a child enters the eighth grade, they will already have spent more than half a million minutes in school classrooms. What they have learnt at school is the sum total of what happened during those half a million minutes. This is not the same as how much they know or can do; that is also influenced by what happened during the 91% of the time since they were born when they were not at school, including a whole range of things which their parents do, whether they went to preschool, and the month of the year in which they were born. When we try to measure all of this in tests, we inevitably get a significant measurement error.

In order to determine how much a child learns during their year with a particular teacher (the 'value added'), we therefore need to start by testing students at the beginning of the year, and then test them again at the end of the year so that we can measure the difference. This does not however solve the problem. First, there are highly significant cumulative and residual effects of teacher quality. A student who had a good teacher in seventh grade will learn more in eighth grade, irrespective of what happens during that year, and vice versa. Second, there may be external events which affect how much a student learns, irrespective of the efforts of the teacher. In 2006, school results in Louisiana plummeted. This of course had nothing to do with the quality of Louisiana's teachers, and though devastating natural disasters are not a typical occurrence, they do exemplify in catastrophic form the smaller events and tragedies which are typical and do affect performance in individual classrooms. Third, and perhaps most importantly, the effects of good teaching may not become apparent in the space of the year. We know that the extent to which a student is engaged, attentive, and behaves well in class is a major determinant of how much they learn. A teacher who spends an entire year helping a student to focus in class may see little additional learning during that year, but has laid a foundation for years to come. In many schools, these problems of measuring teacher effects are compounded by the fact that students often have several teachers. Even if all of those issues could be addressed, there is still a broader set of limitations associated with testing already discussed above, particularly the fact that it necessarily addresses only a small number of the outcomes which are important, and the fact that even the best tests have a large measurement error.

The third problem, which is caused in part by the preceding two, is that pay-for-performance is often extremely unpopular among teachers. As a result, introducing a pay-for-performance scheme is likely to eat considerably into the time, energy, and political capital of the leadership of the school system trying to introduce it. Given the limited benefits of the schemes, it is unlikely that introducing a pay-for-performance scheme would be the best possible use of limited political capital and leadership time. Moreover, it may sour relations with teachers, making it much harder to implement the reforms that would lead to improvements in teaching and learning. A school system which prioritised reforms by asking 'how much benefit will this bring to the children in our schools' would already be performing very well by the time it got round to implementing a pay-for-performance structure.

These problems are not unique to education. Numerous private sector organizations have experimented with pay-for-performance schemes in similar contexts only to drop them for similar reasons.

During the 1990s, thirteen separate business units at Hewlett Packard experimented with merit-pay systems. Within three years, all of the schemes had been dropped. The schemes were difficult to design in a way that captured the complexity of the different dimensions of performance that the company wanted, and had negative effects which outweighed the benefits. "Managers at each site eventually concluded that they could attain greater performance benefits through alternative managerial tools like effective leadership, clear objectives, coaching, or training, and therefore discontinued their pay for performance programs."[42] In the words of one review: "[Often] the real problem is that incentives work too well. Specifically, they motivate employees to focus excessively on doing what they need to do to gain rewards, sometimes at the expense of doing other things that would help the organization. ... When performance evaluation is based on judgment, managers (or peers) do not like to differentiate between employees, fearing damaged relations and de-motivation. When it is not, incentives systems narrow perspective and reduce commitment to the total enterprise."[43]

As a result of those problems, most school systems will struggle to implement a pay-for-performance system, and are unlikely to see a positive benefit it they do, particularly if they are not already performing reasonably well. However, there are a few cases in which pay-for-performance may help to improve outcomes from the school system.

The first is that in some developing-world school systems, where schools are widely distributed geographically and where teacher motivation is very low, pay-for-performance may be the best way to ensure that students at least master some basic skills. These are not school systems where some teachers demonstrate poorer pedagogical skills that others; these are systems where teachers may not even bother to attend school for weeks on end. In India, a study consisting of unannounced visits to 3,700 schools in 20 states found that 1 in

4 teachers was absent from school on any given day.[44] Similar levels of absenteeism have been found in a number of African countries.[45] Some schemes linking pay to performance (or at a minimum attendance) have been effective in reducing these rates of absenteeism.[46] However, even in these cases, addressing the root causes of absenteeism and introducing simple systems for monitoring attendance can be just as effective.[47]

The second is that in high-performing school systems with good school leadership, introducing subjective evaluations of teachers linked to pay can be effective. Singapore rates each teacher against a performance matrix which examines both current performance and potential, and uses this as the basis for allocating substantial end-of-year salary bonuses and increments. The performance criteria are broad, and cover both different aspects of teaching quality and the teacher's wider contribution to the school. Teachers in the top performance band receive an annual bonus equivalent to two month's salary. Because the system is underpinned by capable school leaders who's judgement is trusted by individual teachers, and because the criteria against which teachers are evaluated are transparent and carefully designed, the system appears to have become an accepted part of the teaching system and an effective means to rewarded talented and dedicated teachers.

The final exception is that where pay-for-performance schemes are implemented at the level of schools rather than individual teachers (for instance, as a bonus given to a school that performs well to be distributed among the whole staff) the chances of them succeeding are higher. Because of the larger number of students involved, estimates of the effectiveness of individual schools based on assessment or review are much more accurate than estimates of the effectiveness of individual teachers. They also have the benefit of incentivizing the teachers in a school to work together to raise their collective performance rather than singling out individuals who are performing below average. New York City recently piloted a scheme whereby schools which meet their performance targets receive a bonus equivalent to $3,000 for each staff member. Compensation committees within the school can decide to divide the bonus equally among staff or to recognise individual contributions with higher rewards. Unlike many other attempts to introduce performance-based pay in schools, the scheme received strong backing from local teachers unions, and appears to have been successful in its first year.

Review and assessments are most effective when combined with determined professionalism

Standards, assessment, and review, when implemented effectively, can have a strong positive effect on performance in a school system. However, the extent to which that effect is achieved depends entirely on the extent to which teachers and schools are willing and able to make the changes necessary to improve performance. This fact is the basis of a frequently-articulated argument that assessment and review are themselves redundant; that school systems would do better to rely solely on the professionalism and leadership of teachers and schools to drive improvement. The argument is supported by the many examples of schools and teachers which have high expectations of their students in systems which set low expectations, and the many examples of the reverse. The best teachers hold themselves accountable through their own drive, passion, and professionalism, and the best principals create that sense of mission, drive, and accountability among their entire school staff. Ultimately, those forms of internally-driven accountability are far more powerful that the effect of external assessments or reviews.

That argument, however, ignores the possibility that their combined effect of the two may be more powerful than either one alone. The best companies in the private sector thrive on a combination of two: the internal drive, commitment, and passion of their people fused with the external pressures of a competitive market, demanding customers, and a challenging and rapidly changing environment. Likewise, the best schools thrive on the combination of their own drive to get every student to learn combined with the challenge imposed by tough external standards. Moreover, the absence of that challenge can be damaging to the whole system if it allows a small minority of schools and teachers who lack their own sense of commitment to fail to provide a good education to students over a long period of time.

If challenge from the system is most effective when it is combined with determined professionalism and high expectations from schools and teachers themselves, it is also amplified when the structure of the school system – the way in which it is organized – supports them to develop and improve. The next chapter looks at how decisions about the structure of the school system affect its performance.

6.

A tale of two cities

(Markets, monopolies, and getting the structure right)

How a school system is structured – the way in which rights, responsibilities, powers, and budgets are distributed within it – has a substantial bearing on both its performance and its ability to improve. Good structures achieve three often conflicting objectives: they empower people to perform their roles effectively and innovate where necessary, they hold them accountable for performance, and they encourage the spread of good practice and effective leadership across large numbers of schools. There are no unique structural solutions which will achieve those three objectives; both centralized state-run school systems and diverse markets of competing independent schools can achieve all three when organized well. However, most school systems, whether centralized or decentralized, are structured in ways that fail to provide the best conditions for performance and improvement, and few structural reforms have come close to producing the results their designers intended. In practice, both great attention to detail and innovative approaches to creating links between schools are required to get the structure right.

Different structures, similar outcomes
On almost every indicator of student performance, Singapore and Hong Kong score among the top in the world. When students in the two school systems are tested in international assessments, their performance is often indistinguishable. The contexts in which their school systems operate are also relatively similar: both countries trace a long Asian cultural heritage, they are of similar size (Hong Kong

is about 30% larger, both in terms of its population and its land area), both had a strong British colonial influence which shaped the structure and curriculum of the school system, both used British A-levels and O-Levels as the main school qualification for most of their history, and both are small economies dependent on a similar mix of service, financial, and trading industries.

Structurally, their school systems could not be more different. Singapore's school system is highly centralized. Teachers are recruited and trained centrally, allocated to schools by the Ministry and evaluated against a single performance matrix. Principals are selected trained and evaluated directly by the Ministry of Education and the National Institute of Education. Many aspects of school life, curriculum, and practices are determined by centrally-defined policies or guidance, though teachers and principals have control over teaching in their own schools and the freedom to deviate from many policies when appropriate.

In Hong Kong, by contrast, 95% of students are educated in privately-operated schools which receive funding from the government. Schools have autonomy in almost every significant aspect of their operation: they hire, train, and evaluate their own teachers, form their own budgets, and have considerable influence over curriculum. Principals are selected by private school boards. There are relatively few central regulations and policies, and the Ministry has little control over the operation of individual schools. Yet despite the striking structural differences between it and Singapore, its performance is remarkably similar, with consistently high achievement, a low incidence of school failure, and good improvement.

That is not to say that structure is unimportant. How a school system is structured has a substantial bearing on both its performance and its ability to improve. It affects choices about who becomes a teacher, who becomes a principal, how decisions are made about resources, and how people are held accountable for performance. It affects the extent to which good practices are able to move between schools and the extent to which schools and teachers have the ability both to try new approaches and to repeat old mistakes. However, though the structure of the system is important, there do not appear to be any specific structural arrangements which produce high performance in schools; both highly centralized state-run school systems and school systems in which many independent schools compete is a free market can be highly successful. Moreover, simply changing the structure of the system only rarely leads to improvements in performance. These same observations are true in the business world as well, where a basic principle of organization is that "strategy rarely dictates unique structural solutions,"[1] and where very different organizational structures can be successful in similar circumstances.

However, like high-performing companies, good school systems do share a set of structural features which explain some of their performance. In particular, they tend to be structured so that they:

- empower people to perform their roles effectively and innovate where necessary;
- hold them accountable for performance, rewarding success and tackling failure; and
- encourage the spread of good practice, innovations, and effective leadership across large numbers of schools.

There is an inevitable tension between those three objectives. The more tightly people are held accountable, the less empowered they become; and the more the system is structured to provide for leadership and collaboration between different schools, the less empowered and accountable individual schools become. The tension is sometimes referred to as the 'tight-loose' dilemma: how to create a system which is tight enough to spread and enforce best practice but at the same time loose enough to allow schools to innovate, adapt to their own unique circumstances, and be held genuinely accountable for their results. A few school systems have been broadly successful in achieving that balance. Unfortunately, many have not.

State-run monopolies can produce excellent performance in schools, but only when several conditions are met

The dominant model for providing publicly-funded education is the state-run monopoly.[2] All of the schools in an area, or sometimes an entire country, are run by a single government organization. This organization will normally set the curriculum, recruit, train, and place teachers, select, develop, and evaluate school leaders, and define overall policies for the management of schools. It will probably control much of the spending in the system. There will be a clear hierarchy linking the Minister or Chief Education Officer through to individual teachers (though links in the hierarchy will often prove weaker than those in charge would like). Overall, there is likely to be a high level of uniformity across schools, and even where individual schools have some control over their own operation, the similarities between them will greatly outnumber the differences.

Though sometimes highly successful, the structure is prone to a predictable set of weaknesses. First, there is often little pressure on the system, much less individual schools, to be responsive to the demands of either individual students or the economy and society as a whole. As a result, failure and underperformance are rarely tackled swiftly, if at all. Under a monopoly system, whole schools can fail and be left failing for years without any serious action being taken. Curriculum can be out of date, and remain out of date, for decades.

Second, in the absence of pressures to perform, state monopolies can also be more susceptible to increased political interference and the dominance of supplier interests in the running of schools. In the European Union, teacher strikes are more common in countries where teachers are employed by state or national governments than they are in countries where teachers are employed by individual schools.[3] This is not to suggest that a monopoly system is necessarily in the best interests of teachers. By taking away their ability to choose from a range of employers it disempowers them and forces them to resort to more extreme forms of industrial action and greater regulatory protection in order to defend their interests and assert their views, at times both to the benefit and detriment of their students.

Finally, monopoly structures also tend to constrain innovation and incline towards uniformity in provision. The central leadership of the system are ultimately accountable for the performance of every school in the system, and as a result, are likely to tend be prescriptive and conservative in policy, rather than allowing innovation which carries an inevitable risk of failure. Moreover, because there is a single structure for the entire system, it can be difficult to introduce or experiment with new approaches.

Yet though these problems frequently emerge in school systems which are structured as state-run monopolies, they are not inevitable. Singapore demonstrates that a relatively high level of central control can be used to produce some of the best performance and improvement of any school system in the world. It has systems in place to remove teachers who are not performing (which are used regularly), tackles school failure, proactively manages relations with the teaching profession, and has established means of promoting innovation. Moreover, the relatively centralized structure allows the government to spread best practices quickly through the system, ensure that there are consistently high standards of leadership and management in every school, and centralize some aspects of school management to improve quality and efficiency. Four factors explain why Singapore and a few other state-run monopoly school systems have been successful while most have not.

First, there needs to be strong pressure on the system as a whole to perform and improve. This may come from the sustained attention of political leadership, a strong sense of competition with other school systems, or both. Singapore has constantly made education a national priority, invested a large amount of leadership time in developing it, and is driven by a strong national belief that excellent schooling is critical to the success of a country with few resources other than the capabilities of its workforce. Similarly, South Korea's centralized school system has performed well in part because of sustained leadership attention (the Minister of Education has the rank of Deputy Prime Minister), and in part because education is seen as pivotal to national survival. Conversely, other East Asian countries which have centralized school systems but have not invested the same level of political energy into developing them have not reached the same levels of performance.

Second, there needs to be objective monitoring of standards through an independent review or assessment body. Standards in Singapore's examinations have long been externally-moderated through a partnership with a subsidiary of the University of Cambridge in the United Kingdom, and are now administered by an independent examination board in Singapore. Similarly, towns and districts in the Canadian province of Alberta, which has one of the highest levels of performance in the world, generally have local monopolies on schooling, however they are held to account through standards and assessments set and administered by the provincial government. Those arrangements ensure that while the school system has a monopoly on provision, it does not also have a monopoly on judging the quality of that provision.

Third, substantial autonomy needs to be granted to individual schools. Monopoly structures in schooling are frequently accompanied by over-centralization, over-prescription, and excessive central planning, which together make it difficult for individual teachers and schools to go about their work. In many Middle Eastern countries, for instance, school leaders and teachers have almost no control over the curriculum, the organization of teaching and learning, or the management of school staff, making it difficult to raise performance or adapt to local needs.

However, the fact that all schooling is provided by a single organization should not prevent that organization for delegating much control to the front line. In the business sector, the top-performing companies tend to be those which empower their front-line staff and reduce their central administration to the minimum: as one study noted, excellent companies "intentionally keep their [central] staff small. Then there aren't enough [central] staff around to generate too much confusion down the line. Emerson, Schlumberger and Dana, for example, are all [multi-billion dollar] corporations; yet each is run with fewer than 100 bodies in corporate headquarters. ... Rene McPherson, when he took over at Dana, dramatically threw out 22.5 inches of policy manuals and replaced them with a one-page statement of philosophy."[4]

The same tendency to keep central administration small and devolve powers to schools is characteristic of successful monopoly-model school systems. International comparisons show that irrespective of the overall structure of the system, schools which have control over how they organize teaching and learning and how they use resources perform better than those which do not.[5] One Canadian superintendent in a district which had devolved control over spending to the schools noted that "before every school got the same number of everything. It was based on formula. You got X number of teachers based on how many students you had. You got X number of library books based on how many students you had. You had X number of caretakers based on how many students you had. Everything was done by a formula by somebody downtown who knew very little about the students in the schools. We asked, 'What if the teachers in the school know the students better than some functionary who works downtown? What if each of the schools in Edmonton is different from each other?' ... Initially teachers and other staff were really worried this was going to end the world as they knew it. But once the schools got the money and the authority that goes with spending that money, staff said, "This makes a lot of sense." … For example, in a situation where a school wanted and needed to improve reading results in their school they were able to ensure that each teacher recruited for that school brought with them excellent training in the area of reading. So schools started spending the money in a way that made sense for their community and the nature of the students being served."[6]

In Singapore, individual schools have substantial autonomy to plan their own teaching and learning and manage their own resources. In addition, 10% of the schools in the system are designated as independent or autonomous schools. These schools are exempt from many of the Ministry's regulations. Independent schools, for instance, can develop their own curricula, hire their own staff, manage their own resources, and can create partnerships with external organizations. The schools are granted these autonomies to ensure that within an otherwise centralized system there is space for schools to develop new practices and methods which may contradict existing regulations. The dual-system balances the benefits of standardization across the system, which allows best-practices to be deployed quickly across all schools, with the need to innovate and experiment with new practices in order to push forward the frontiers of performance.

Finally, for a monopoly system to work, communication between schools and the central administration needs to be strong. One of the core principles of Toyota's management philosophy is *genchi genbutsu*: "go and see for yourself to thoroughly understand the situation."[7] Toyota's managers are expected to spend much of their time understanding the business at the front line. Hewlett Packard's management style is based on a similar philosophy, enshrined in what the company calls MBWA, "Management By Walking Around." For a school system with a relatively high level of central control to perform well demands that those making decisions at the central office have an excellent understanding of the schools which they are making decisions about. New York's current chancellor, responsible for the running of more than 1,000 schools, chose to locate his office in the middle of a school. Singapore rotates Ministry officials between central-office postings and secondments to individual schools to ensure that they have a strong understanding of the realities of the school environment. In most cases, successful monopoly school systems seem to be those which have a no more than a few hundred schools contained within a relatively small geographic area, facilitating a high level of interaction between the schools and the centre, though there is no particular reason why a larger monopoly could not be successful given the right organizational structure.

In essence, monopoly models appear to be successful where there is sufficient external pressure on the system to drive performance, and where they are structured in ways which empower individuals and schools to perform their roles effectively and innovate where necessary, hold people accountable for performance, and encourage collaboration, the spread of best practice, innovations, and leadership across large numbers of schools. In many instances however, monopoly models have failed to create those conditions, and as a result, policymakers have looked to alternative models for organizing the school system.

The most widely supported alternative to the monopoly model is to make individual schools independent organizations which compete for students

The most widely supported and commonly implemented alternative to the monopoly structure is to make each school independent and give parents the right to choose between them. Schools become individual organizations, free to hire their own staff, develop their own budgets, policies, and plans, and held accountable by the communities which they serve. Parents can choose any school for their children, with funding going to the school of their choice. The model is often called a market model of education, because it harnesses market forces of choice and competition to drive improvement. Probably the most dramatic example of transition from a monopoly to a market model, is a school reform implemented in New Zealand in 1989 called 'Tomorrow's Schools.'

Until September 1989, New Zealand's public school system was run on a monopoly model. The Department of Education, led by its Director General, managed the country's 2,700 schools from its offices in Wellington through a network of regional and local boards. The Department recruited, trained, and evaluated all of New Zealand's teachers, selected its principals, and maintained its schools. Approval from regional offices was required for everything from basic maintenance to teacher training. "Education officials made decisions not only on matters of curriculum and textbooks but also on the number of scissors to which each school was entitled or what colour to paint the gymnasium's walls. ... [As one principal recalled] 'I had to go to four separate departments and get a chit from Wellington to purchase a twelve dollar brush for the bus driver to clean his bus.'"[8] The Department of Education "suffered through the growth over the years of volumes of rules for everything. Decisions seemed to take an interminable time (frequently because they had to be referred to the Minister)."[9]

In response, the government initiated a radical and swift restructuring of the system. At midnight on Saturday 30 September 1989, the Department of Education ceased to exist. It was replaced by a new and smaller Ministry of Education with a completely new senior staff: "only one person from the top three tiers of the old Department won a senior post in the new Ministry."[10] Schools became independent, each accountable to its own board of trustees and with full control of a delegated budget. Each school was responsible for recruiting its staff, training its teachers, developing or purchasing its curriculum, maintaining its facilities, controlling its spending, and ultimately, providing a quality education to its students. A new independent inspection agency, the Education Review Office, was established to monitor standards in schools. "Virtually overnight … one of the world's most tightly controlled public educational systems became one of the most decentralized."[11]

The design of the New Zealand reforms combined three major ideas about the management of schools, which together make up the market model. It devolved substantial powers to individual schools giving each school a budget linked to the number of students it enrolled and a high degree of freedom over how that money was spent (often referred to as school-based management). It made schools accountable to their local communities through boards of trustees elected by the parents of children enrolled in the school, rather than having them directly accountable to the government. These boards would approve the budget, select, evaluate, and, where necessary, remove the principal, and participate in making important decisions about the running of the school. Finally, it introduced choice and competition into the system. After the first two years, parents could choose any school for their children, subject to capacity constraints, with public funds following the student to that school. A school's budget, and in theory its overall viability, would depend on its ability to attract students.

While all three of those ideas are essential elements of a market model, they do not necessarily have to go together. Singapore, for instance, has introduced some elements of school-based management and parental choice of schools in the context of an otherwise centralized system. However, most countries have tended to implement the three together. England implemented a market-based structure for its school system through the Education Act of 1988. The Arabian Gulf state of Qatar is gradually converting government schools to independent status, though schools will be held accountable through a contract with the government rather than through elected boards of parents. Other school systems – for instance Hong Kong, Ireland, and the Netherlands – have evolved historically as market-model systems of independent publicly-funded schools. Each of these school systems differs, particularly with regard to how much freedom is granted to individual schools (for instance, how strictly teacher qualifications or curriculum are controlled) and what types of organization are eligible to receive public funding for education (for instance, whether for-profit companies can operate publicly-funded schools, or whether private schools which charge additional fees can be eligible for public funding), however the basic principles of schools operating independently, local accountability, and competition for students are the same.

A few countries have also experimented with hybrid models, where most schools are run through a single government organization, but a few are allowed to operate independently as if they were part of a market system. In the United States, there are now around 4,000 such schools, known as Charter schools, which receive public funding but operate outside the regular district structure and regulations, often with their own boards. They have a broad set of freedoms, including the ability to set their own budgets and employ their own staff, which are granted in return for an agreement on accountability for student performance known as the school 'charter.' In some school systems these models are being used to facilitate a gradual transition from a monopoly to a market model of schooling.

Market-based reforms do not tend to lead to improvements in student outcomes

Unfortunately, there is little evidence that introducing market models leads to significant improvements in school performance, and some evidence that they can lead to a decline in equity and other adverse effects. Overall, school systems in which there is competition between schools for students perform about six points higher on PISA – a significant increase, but very small compared to the overall variation in the effectiveness of different schools and school systems.

In many cases where structural change has been implemented there has been little improvement in the overall performance of the system, though often, gaps between the best schools and the worst have become wider as a result of structural change. In New Zealand, many schools improved as a result of the reforms, and a small number launched highly successful changes to their curriculum and teaching which would not have been possible under the old system. However, in large numbers of schools, there was no real change, and in many, teaching and learning deteriorated as a result of the reforms. The government later recognized that "the new system does not work for 10-20 percent of schools, including some entire regions, both urban and rural,"[12] and that up to a third of schools may have deteriorated as a result of the reform. Though there is no clear data with which to assess the impact of the reforms, one study reflected an emerging consensus in concluding that "the question [of whether the reform led to an improvement in teaching and learning] cannot be answered firmly, but a reasonable hypothesis might be 'yes' for some students, 'no significant change' for many, and 'deteriorated' for some."[13]

Similar patterns have emerged in other school systems which have experimented with market models. One American study of three transformations from a monopoly to a market model found that all three districts had "undergone significant organizational changes to facilitate their ambitious instructional improvement plans. The unfortunate reality ... is that districts were unable to change and improve practice on a large scale. And the evidence is indisputable: you can't improve student learning without improving instruction."[14] In Chicago, which implemented a similar reform to

New Zealand in 1988, the outcome was a similar "'story of three-thirds': one third of schools engaged in self-initiated active restructuring, one third struggled with improvement, while one third were left behind."[15] Overall performance stayed roughly the same.

Hybrid models have produced similarly disappointing results. In the United States some of the best charter schools, including KIPP, Green Dot, and Aspire, have used their autonomy to achieve excellent results. However, on average, the mathematics and reading scores of students in charter schools are slightly lower than those in regular district schools, even after correcting for the effect of student background.[16] Given that many charter schools are new schools in their first few years of operation, it might be argued that in the long term they will slightly outperform their public counterparts. Even so, the overall picture is clear; simply giving schools more autonomy or increasing competition and parental choice does not produce reliable improvements in performance.

In response to that evidence, some commentators have argued that competition does not work in education; that for some reason, the incentives which help to drive progress in almost every other sector of the economy are not applicable to schools. That argument is made despite clear examples of cases where competition has been a powerful driver of improvement in individual schools. Other commentators have argued that competition works but only produces improvements over a much longer period of time, even though school systems which have had market models for many years do not seem to perform much better than those which have not. More plausible is the argument that there are deficiencies in the way in which markets have been created in education which limit their ability to drive improvement.

Imagine that the government shut down every coffee shop except for one chain; for instance, imagine that all of the coffee shops were closed except for Starbucks. Then the government told you that you could choose any Starbucks that you wanted, as long as you lived nearby, and it did not already have too many customers, and the Starbucks accepted you as a customer. In some cases, the oversubscribed Starbucks stores would be able to chose their customers, rejecting those with complex drinks orders or who often ordered drinks which were harder to prepare. Having chosen your Starbucks, you would of course only then be able to get coffee at that one store. You and the other customers would be able to elect a board which would have the power to fire the manager of the store, although in practice, this would only happen in the very worst cases, usually when almost no coffee had been produced at all over a period of several years. A small minority of affluent people would be able to buy their way out of this system and get their coffee from a range of private coffee shops. The government would declare this a market because everybody had a choice of which Starbucks to go to, and because individual stores had the freedom to make choices about how best to serve their products, although the menu and prices would be centrally determined by the government.

This is broadly how markets for schools function. As a result, school systems which employ market models tend to suffer a range of problems: they fail to leverage choice and competition as real drivers of improvement, they are unable to quickly or preventively tackle underperformance, they divide the system into units which are too small to innovate, they inhibit the spread of best practices, and they often increase academic, ethnic, and social stratification in the system. More fundamentally, the power of choice and competition as drivers of improvement has generally been overstated.

In theory a market model allows parents to choose their child's school, and in doing so, preference good schools over bad creating a force for improvement. In a few cases this works well. In Hong Kong, for instance, parents are able to choose which school their children attend through a part-lottery system. The small size of the country, its dense population, and its excellent transport system mean that parents have a genuine choice of almost any school in the city. Moreover, because the overall size of the school population is declining, schools are closed on a regular basis. Parental choice means that the lowest-performing schools – more than 10% of all schools over the past ten years – are unable to attract sufficient students and are ultimately closed. This means that there is genuine pressure on schools to improve and a real exit from the market for those schools which do not.

However, in most cases, choice has proven to be a very weak driver of improvement. For instance, under the No Child Left Behind legislation in the United States, parents receive regular information about the performance of their child's school and have the right to transfer their children to another school if their school is under-performing. However, in practice, parents rarely exercise that right. In Los Angeles, only 215 out of 204,000 children who were eligible to change school under No Child Left Behind actually transferred.[17] Across the United States as a whole, less than 1% of the 3.9 million students eligible to transfer out of failing schools exercised that option.[18] There are many reasons why this is the case. Parents tend to have a strong preference for schools which are close to where they live – particularly if there is a 'neighbourhood school' which most of the local kids attend. In the vast majority of cases there are no real options to transfer schools, either because good schools are already over-subscribed, or because there are no good schools in the area. In other cases, parents of children simply do not want to go through the process of transferring and settling into a new school, or regulations make transferring between schools a difficult if not impossible task. Finally, parents of children in under-performing schools often have low expectations of schools and a tendency to believe that the quality of education their children are getting is better than it actually is. "[When a] school is poor, the evidence suggests that ... parents are even more likely to rally around it. Generations of chief education officers have discovered that the one guaranteed means of generating parental support for a school is to propose its closure."[19]

These problems are more acute in school systems which lack good publicly-available information on the performance of individual schools. The PISA surveys show that parents in school systems where there is no public reporting on the performance of schools do not tend to make accurate judgements about how well their children's schools are performing.[20] In those systems, schools which parents thought were good actually performed at exactly the same level as those which they thought were bad. Conversely, in systems where data on performance is made public, schools which parents think are good do perform better than other schools. Data from England collected before school performance data was made public show that while students often made accurate judgements about the quality of their school and the teaching in it, parents tended to be satisfied with their school, even when signs of failure were apparent.[21] As a result, in the absence of good information about the performance of schools, market models and choice are unlikely to lead to improvements in performance.

A further complication of choice is that it can lead to an increase in academic and social stratification if careful controls on admissions are not enforced. Where a society is divided along racial or confessional lines, parents will tend to choose schools where their own confessional or racial group is in the majority, leading to increased segregation. In New Zealand, students in mixed areas tended to self-select into 'white' and 'Maori' schools.[22] "In the five years following the introduction of parental choice ... students sorted themselves out by ethnic group and to a lesser extent by socioeconomic status to a degree that cannot be explained by changes in ethnic and demographic residential patterns."[23] Similar effects have been found in

Northern Ireland, Lebanon, and some urban school systems in the United States.

In addition, the devolved nature of the system makes it more difficult to prevent school failure or tackle it quickly once it has occurred. In New Zealand, a substantial number of schools failed during the first years of the reform, but the government, having fully delegated control to the school level, was powerless to do anything. Only after an amendment was passed to the Education Act in 2001 was central government able to intervene in cases of school failure. Since then, New Zealand and other market-based systems such as England have developed more effective means of tackling school failure when it occurs. However, even now, both governments lack the power to intervene pre-emptively to prevent school failure, even when they have clear evidence that a decline in performance is imminent, and know how that decline can be avoided. In contrast, well-run monopoly systems can prevent schools from failing in the first place by intervening as soon as the signs of a fall in performance emerge.

At the same time, overall improvement is made more difficult by the high level of fragmentation in the system. England, for instance, now has more than 25,000 individual competing schools, many of which have fewer than one hundred students. That level of fragmentation is higher than in any comparable industry, and means that few schools have the scale necessary to innovate, invest in developing new practices, or extract economies of scale. Even when innovation does occur or best practices do emerge, the high level of fragmentation makes it harder for that innovation to spread between schools. Rather, innovation and good practice tend to stay within the schools where they are developed because relationships between schools are weak, there is no super-school leadership to drive the spread of good practices, and schools are in competition with each other incentivizing them to hold on to good practice or talented teachers rather than dedicate a part of their time to helping other schools. In New Zealand, one evaluation of the reform noted that "while there were some exciting pockets of change, they remained pockets."[24] After the reform "principals and teachers became less willing to share pedagogical and other ideas with their counterparts at schools with which their school is competing for students."[25]

A final failing of the market model as implemented in some school systems is that it generally does little to enable or incentivize the best schools to expand quickly, or to takeover and transform other schools. In theory, good schools should be able to attract more students, expand, and thereby increase the number of students receiving a good education, just as good businesses expand and take customers away from other companies with less developed products and services. Ironically, in a few school systems, the market structure actually encourages good schools to take as few students as possible. In New Zealand, the Ministry of Education decides on the maximum number of students that each school is able to accommodate. Once schools reach that capacity, they can cap their student intake, and then have the right to choose which students they admit. Once they start selecting their own students, their performance goes up because they are able to accept students who are performing better to begin with. That in turn drives applications even higher. The system incentivizes them to stay small and selective in order to maintain that high performance rather than expanding and thereby lowering the average ability of their incoming class, and consequently their overall performance. The gap between their performance and that of other schools widens, often enabling them to attract the best teachers as well, and making it more difficult for those other schools to catch up. Once the performance gap is large enough, it also reduces the pressure on those other schools to improve further, because they are already so far behind that they stand little chance of catching up. In New Zealand, "the system quickly flip-flopped in some fast-growing urban areas from one in which parents and children choose schools to one in which schools choose students."[26]

All of those problems can be overcome in a good market system. For instance, schools can be allowed to form larger federations or networks to overcome the barriers of fragmentation and enable them to learn from each other. In the United States several chains of charter schools have emerged, some of which now have more than 50 schools. Those chains, on average, outperform both independent charter schools and the public school system as a whole.[27] In Sweden, chains of publicly-funded privately-managed schools outperform other schools and have led innovation and improvement across the system as a whole.[28] In England and elsewhere, the Specialist Schools and Academies Trust has facilitated cooperation, networking, and the spread of best practices between secondary schools in an otherwise highly fragmented school system. Several Canadian provinces have led the way in finding ways to encourage and facilitate cooperation between schools: for instance, by pairing principals of schools with the best record of improvement with those finding improvement more difficult. Good policies on admissions, public transportation of students to schools, and the opening and closing of new schools can make choice a real driver of improvement, and good data and interventions to support schools which start to fail can prevent devolution of powers to schools from leading to an increase in the incidence and severity of school failure. However, as currently implemented, few market models do all of those things, and as a result, their performance has often been no better than that of monopoly based systems.

How a school system is structured greatly affects both its performance and its capacity to improve. However, like standards and assessment, structural reforms have often been seen as a magic wand to improve performance, or as a means of avoiding the need to tackle the real problems of poor teaching and school management. In fact, while structural reform may enable other changes, it rarely improves performance in and of itself. Destroying large bureaucracies or cutting schools loose from the system can be a simple and politically attractive choice for policymakers, but one that often fails to address the root causes of underperformance. In particular, no structure will ever produce good teaching and learning in schools in the absence of good school leaders and good teachers. The next chapter looks at ways to improve the skills and knowledge of the teaching workforce itself.

7.

Into the Middle Kingdom

(Building teachers' professional knowledge and skills)

A school system can have excellent people, leaders, standards, and structures, but unless its teachers have the knowledge and skills to help every child to learn, it will never perform well. Compared to other professions and some organizations, many school systems have been remarkably unsuccessful both at preparing new teachers for entry into the profession and at helping all teachers to access the skills and knowledge of the best. However a few schools systems, particularly in Asia, have developed good models for ensuring that teachers have the knowledge and skills they need to be effective in the classroom. They do that by making sure that teachers have a sound grasp of the content which they are teaching, providing them with a strong foundation of pedagogical knowledge, and, most importantly, by providing them with multiple opportunities to acquire tacit knowledge and practical skills from experienced teachers in schools.

Student outcomes depend on teachers being able to acquire a substantial body of professional knowledge, skills, and values

One way of thinking about the performance of a school system is to imagine it as the sum of the quality of teaching and learning in its classrooms. In part, that quality depends on getting the right people to become teachers and on creating schools and systems which enable them to perform well once they enter the classroom. However, the quality of teaching and learning in classrooms and schools ultimately rests on the capabilities of individual teachers. Any improvement in the performance of a school system ultimately implies an improvement in the skills and knowledge of the teachers working in it; or as one management expert counsels: "before people [and organizations] can improve, they first must learn."[1] Ensuring that teachers are able to learn lies at the core of the role of any school system: "You could define the entire task of [a school] system in this way: its role is to ensure that when a teacher enters the classroom he or she has the materials available, along with the knowledge, the capability, and the ambition, to take one more child up to the standard today than she did yesterday."[2]

Good teaching is grounded in a highly complex set of skills and knowledge. Teachers need a strong understanding of the material they are teaching, the strategies for teaching it, the different obstacles or pitfalls that can block student learning, the ability to assess how well students are learning and identify issues, and the capacity to deliver that material in a way that is appropriate to individual students, sustains their attention, and manages the distractions and problems that can arise in the classroom. One review of mathematics teaching underscores well the complexity of effective teaching: "The best teaching was rooted in developing pupils' understanding of key concepts. It was inclusive in terms of ensuring that all pupils made substantial progress, no matter what their starting points. In the outstanding lessons, the teachers had high expectations of pupils' enjoyment and achievement. They made conscious efforts to foster a spirit of enquiry, developing pupils' reasoning skills through approaches that saw problem-solving and investigation as integral to learning mathematics. They checked that everyone was challenged to think hard and they adapted how they were teaching to achieve this. As a result, their classrooms were vibrant places of learning. In the most effective lessons, teachers often presented new topics by challenging pupils to apply their mathematics to solve problems, drawing ideas from them and using probing questions to gauge their initial understanding and develop it. They sequenced learning carefully, helping pupils to make links to related areas of mathematics. They used visual aids and demonstrated ways of thinking that helped pupils to understand the methods they were learning and to overcome common misconceptions. The teachers listened to pupils carefully and observed their work throughout the lesson. They aimed to identify any potential misconceptions or barriers to understanding key concepts, and responded accordingly."[3]

Many commentators have argued that teacher education and professional development are of little value in helping to develop those skills. Some argue that excellent teachers are born not made; that the talents required to teach well are intrinsic to certain individuals, not potential outcomes of effective training and development. This is certainly true to a degree, and is the basis for the argument for selecting the right people to become teachers in chapter three. Others argue that acquiring those skills is fundamentally an individual journey of discovery through trial, error, and experimentation. Both arguments reflect a substantial body of evidence showing that trained teachers often perform little better than those who have received no formal training.[4] Not only does training appear to have little effect, there is also evidence that heavy requirements for initial teacher training can reduce the quality of applicants to teaching, because good candidates are deterred by lengthy training requirements.[5]

However, in general, those findings about the limited impact of teacher training are more a reflection of the inadequacy of existing training programs than a reflection of the futility of training itself. The research does ultimately show that teachers depend on a common set of skills and knowledge, and that those skills and knowledge can be developed more consistently and to a higher standard through effective training that by mere trial and error. There is clear evidence that new teachers who receive good training during their first years teaching perform better than those who do not,[6] and that new teachers who do not receive good training and support are more likely to leave teaching during the first few years. Teachers themselves say that good professional development is important to improving their performance in the classroom, particularly during the early stages of their careers.[7] There are also good examples of school systems which have achieved substantial improvements in student outcomes through effective professional development for teachers.[8] And there are a few school systems which demonstrate that strong development practices throughout the system can produce consistently high performance and improvement. Unfortunately, those examples are in the minority.

Most school systems have been remarkably unsuccessful both at preparing new teachers and at helping all teachers to access the skills and knowledge of the best

Though developing the capacity of the teaching workforce is arguably the single most important function of a school system, few of the world's school systems have found ways to build that capacity consistently throughout the teaching workforce. While there are some examples of good practice in every school system, in most, professional development is undertaken mainly in ways which have long been known to be ineffective.[9] Ironically, much professional development for teachers is characterized by the very approaches – lecture-style teaching, a lack of opportunities for trainees to immediately apply what they are learning, and poor matching of training and the needs of the trained – which it seeks to eliminate in those being trained. This is despite a growing understanding of what works and what does not: as one expert notes, "professional development is one of those areas in which our knowledge of what to do and how to do it exceeds our demonstrated capacity to act on that knowledge."[10] More specifically, most training fails to improve classroom performance for three main reasons.

First, in most training programs, theories of teaching and learning tend to dominate knowledge about how to apply them. Teachers can be more effective when they have a good theoretical understanding of how students learn, the different ways to support that learning, and the different problems that can arise in the process. However, far more important, and far more difficult, is teaching teachers to apply that theoretical understanding in their classrooms. Evaluations of different training activities show that the ones which teachers find more useful, and the ones which have the most impact on classroom practice, are those which support teachers to improve practice in their classrooms.[11] Yet in most school systems, training of teachers focuses mainly on theory to the exclusion of extended efforts to support teachers in applying it.[12] In the United States, for instance, many programs to train new teachers include "only a cursory knowledge of how to teach reading skills,"[13] despite the fact that making sure that every child can read is one of the main priorities for any school system. In several wealthy Middle Eastern countries, teacher training includes no courses on how to teach reading, and, as a result, children in those countries have much lower levels of reading achievement that children in countries with a comparable education spending which do train their teachers to teach reading.[14] Even once teachers are serving in schools, professional development often consists mainly of workshops, lectures, or further academic study with only a small applied component. This is not to suggest that those cannot be important forms of professional development, but rather that they cannot be the only or even the prime means of supporting teachers to develop their skills.

Second, and more importantly, there are normally too few opportunities for teachers to practice what they are learning with the support of a more experienced teacher. This is important, because most of the knowledge and skills which good teachers demonstrate cannot be captured in words or on paper, and even if they could, reading or hearing those words would not make a new teacher an excellent practitioner. As one expert counsels large businesses: the "best employees' deepest knowledge can't be transferred onto a series of PowerPoint slides or downloaded into a data repository. It has to be passed on in person – slowly, patiently, and systematically."[15] Like other professionals, much of the knowledge which teachers require to be effective is best described as *tacit* knowledge, "the things we know but cannot tell." An experienced professional "develops a wealth of experience ... but he is often unable to articulate the scientific or technical principles behind what he knows. ... It consists of mental models, beliefs, and perspectives so ingrained that we take them for granted."[16] That knowledge can only be passed on through modelling, coaching, and apprenticeship in schools, not through books and lectures.

While most new teachers undertake some teaching practice as part of their initial training, and many school systems now have limited induction programs, that practical coaching still tends to form only a small part of a much longer training program. In most cases, training takes place mainly in universities and lecture halls with little connection to the schools and classrooms in which teachers will later teach. That is in contrast to every other profession, and a few of the best school systems, where a large component of both initial and on-going training is carried out through apprenticeship and coaching in the classroom. It denies teachers the opportunities to develop the practical skills and values which can only be developed in an authentic setting, and creates a context in which training can easily become detached from the reality of practice or fail to adapt to changing curricula and practices. When trainee teachers do spend time in schools as part of their training, they consistently say it is the most valuable part of their course.

Even once teachers begin working full-time in schools, their pro-

fessional development tends to be characterised by the same detach-
ment from the classroom as initial training. In many school systems
it takes place outside the school, or takes the form of workshops or
lectures in schools which, the research suggests, do very little to help
improve teaching practice, and are rarely tailored to the specific
needs of individual teachers or schools. In other school systems,
teachers are encouraged to take master's degrees at university, which
again have little effect on their effectiveness in the classroom.[17] More
than half of teachers in the developed world receive no professional
development at all.[18] The OECD characterises professional development in most school systems as "fragmented, unrelated to teaching
practice, and lacking in intensity and follow-up."[19]

Finally, the quality of the training programs themselves often limits their potential to help teachers develop. Training may be delivered
by people who are not excellent practitioners themselves, which un-
dermines both the quality of training they can give and the credibility with which they give it. Courses are often structured poorly and
do little to evaluate their own effectiveness. Many induction programs have been criticized for focusing on socializing teachers rather
than developing their practical skills, are delivered by coaches or
mentors with little or no experience in coaching or mentoring, and
are disconnected from prior or subsequent phases or training.

Interestingly, the approach used to train teachers contrasts greatly
with the approach taken to training and development by almost
every other profession, and by most major companies. For instance,
since reforms ushered in following the publication of the Flexner
Report in 1910, medical education has consistently adopted approaches very different from those used to develop teachers. Training
of new doctors involves a constant blending of the theoretical and
the practical, with medical students undertaking years of guided
practice in parallel to their academic studies. That practice seeks to
build both the skills that doctors need and also the mindsets, values,

and professionalism that underpin good practice. It is undertaken mainly in teaching hospitals, which are both fully functioning hospitals and places of learning. It is delivered by practicing doctors who are, in general, among the best in their fields. It is grounded in both a rigorous preparation in the content-knowledge of medicine and an environment which provides constant intellectual challenge. Finally, it delivered to a consistent model and set of quality standards irrespective of the individual institution an aspiring doctor attends. As one superintendent notes: "we would never turn out a freshly minted doctor and say, 'go operate on somebody' without three or four years of practice – guided practice. Practice with supervision. Practice with pressure. Practice with support. Practice with a lead doctor. But we turn out teachers, put them in rooms, [and] ignore them."[20]

As a result, many new teachers, and some experienced teachers, lack the skills and knowledge to teach effectively, and many become demoralized and leave teaching early as a result. In the United States, "14 percent of teachers leave the classroom in the first year, [and] nearly half by the fifth year."[21] Research studies find that new teachers who have completed long periods of pre-service teacher training perform no better than those who have not,[22] and link both poor teaching skills and high teacher attrition to a lack of effective professional development. One review in Australia noted that "if preparedness for teaching was the criterion applied in any explicit sense to answer the question whether university programmes were satisfactory, schools where new graduates were employed would be hard to convince that they were."[23] "Put simply, many new teachers seem to lack practical teaching skills, as opposed to the theoretical foundations required to be an effective teacher."[24]

Yet a few school systems have found ways to train new teachers effectively. Many use approaches that closely resemble training and development in other professions and the private sector. In particular, one of the main drivers of the high-performance of several East Asian school systems has been their phenomenal success in developing new and existing teachers. Similar approaches characterise Finland, another top-performer, and a range of improving school systems in other countries. Perhaps the best though, are the schools of Shanghai.

Teachers and professional development in Shanghai

The performance of Shanghai's schools, particularly in mathematics and science, is among the highest in the world. Educationalists familiar with standards in Asian school systems claim that schools in the city have recently pulled ahead of other East Asian leaders in education, including Singapore and Hong Kong, particularly in their teaching of core subjects. Many speculate that Shanghai will pip Singapore, Finland, and the Canadian province of Alberta for the top spot in education league tables when the results of its first participation in the PISA assessments are released at the end of 2010.

In part, Shanghai achieves those results because of a high cultural and economic premium on education. Success in schooling has a greater effect on a person's future prospects and earnings than in many other countries and, as a consequence, students spend more hours studying and come under more pressure to succeed than students in other parts of the world. China also has one of the world's oldest cultural traditions of schooling, examinations, and employment based on educational achievement. However, most commentators attribute its recent success, particularly in relation to other Asian school systems, to the quality of teaching in its schools. Teachers have deeper subject knowledge, greater pedagogical knowledge, and stronger teaching skills than teachers in other school systems. That, in turn, is the product of a highly effective system for preparing and developing its teachers.

New teachers start their training at university. Degrees programs for prospective teachers focus on providing them with a strong understanding of the curriculum they will teach. For instance, training of aspiring primary mathematics teachers concentrates on developing a deep understanding of the mathematics in the primary curriculum, with particular attention paid to areas of the curriculum that are critical to developing a student's understanding of mathematics, areas where students most commonly encounter difficulties, and the different strategies for overcoming those difficulties. Subject training is complemented by courses in pedagogy and a short period of teaching practice.

However, the main period of development for new teachers occurs during the first year after they have completed their university studies. New teachers teach full time in schools, but with intensive coaching and support from experienced teachers focused on developing the professional values, pedagogical knowledge, and practical skills which they need to be effective. Each is assigned a mentor who helps plan lessons, observes classes, and provides feedback and advice, normally several times a week. Mentors are selected from the best teachers in the school, educators who are "regarded as strong, with the ability to articulate their reflections on practice and connect their teaching to principles."[25] The mentoring role is a position of prestige within the school for which teachers are paid an additional stipend.

Their coaching is complemented by a range of other activities. New teachers observe lessons taught by more experienced colleagues and participate in weekly sessions to discuss and plan teaching. They spend half a day a week in formal training outside the school with the rest of their cohort focused on practical aspects of how to teach and organized to meet specific needs that the new teachers are encountering. They participate in regular area-wide teaching competitions and discussions of instructional practice, and are provided with regular opportunities to observe teaching in other schools.

At the end of the year, all new teachers are evaluated against a range of criteria. The school is responsible for assessing their professionalism and adherence to the values expected of teachers. The local district evaluates their teaching skills and performance in the classroom. And their knowledge of their subjects and pedagogy is examined by the municipality through a series of city-wide tests. Those teachers who pass the evaluation become fully-certified teachers. Those who do not are normally given an additional year of support to reach the required standard.

On completion of their first year, new teachers spend a further five years as junior teachers. During that time, they become part of a broader culture of professional development and learning within their schools. Weekly joint sessions for planning and reflection form the core of professional development, with teachers using test data and their own observations to jointly analyse what is working and what is not. Teachers are required to observe their colleagues' teaching on an ongoing basis and provide feedback and advice. Regular demonstration lessons and other public displays of teaching provide a forum for the discussion of teaching practice. The best teachers in each school are recognized as such and play a key role in developing the rest of the staff.

Shanghai's professional development is characterized by a focus on developing both deep subject and pedagogical knowledge and the skills to apply it in the classroom. It provides a range of opportunities for experienced teachers to pass knowledge and skills on to more junior teachers. It treats teaching as a public activity, to be shown, observed, and criticised by others. However, most importantly, it places developing teaching skills at the core of each school's daily activity. Michael Fullan argues that improving performance in schools demands that teachers and schools learn continuously as part of their daily lives; that in the best schools and other organizations, "learning is the work."[26] Of course, neither the integration of professional learning into the daily work of teachers, nor the processes by which that is achieved, are unique to Shanghai. The approach has proven effective in a number of other school systems operating in a range of cultural contexts. Among them is the island of Cuba.

Similar approaches to those used in Shanghai have proved effective elsewhere

During the late 1990s, the United Nations began a project to develop the first international assessment of educational performance in Latin America. Between June and November of 1997 they ran tests in language and mathematics in eleven different South and Central American countries. The results, released in 1998, showed that educational standards in Latin American countries were broadly similar, but with one major exception.[27]

Students in Cuba, one of the poorest countries participating in the tests, performed far ahead of their peers in other countries. The performance of the bottom 25% of students in Cuba was comparable to the performance of the top 25% of students in other Latin American countries. Average students in Cuba outperformed students in the top 10% in every other participating country. Comparisons with other international tests suggest that the educational achievement of 10-year olds in Cuba, with a GDP per capita of just $4,000, is similar to the top school systems of the developed world.

Cuba's school system is one of the best examples of a monopoly model: every school in the country is publicly funded and centrally managed. It has a strong record of attracting highly-talented individuals to the teaching profession, in part because it pays relatively high salaries and is selective about who becomes a teacher, but also because talented individuals have fewer job opportunities than in other countries. However, its high educational standards are often attributed to its success in developing the capacity of its teaching workforce. The models it uses to develop its teachers share all of the main features of professional development in Shanghai. Initial training is long, and focused on developing a deep knowledge of the school curriculum, the pedagogies to teach it, and the skills and values required to deliver that teaching to a consistently high standard. The entire program is delivered mainly in schools, with intense coaching, support, and guidance from the best teachers in those schools. In schools, teachers spend a large portion of each week working collectively to analyse, plan, and improve their teaching.[28] Training and daily activities in the school are all engineered to improve teaching and learning in the classroom.

Other school systems using those approaches have registered significant improvements in teaching and learning as a result. England improved the skills of new teachers by shifting the centre of teacher training from universities to schools, requiring that teachers on one-year postgraduate courses spend two thirds of their training time in schools. The shift in focus was combined with rigorous performance management of training providers to improve the quality of delivery. Training providers were inspected regularly against a set of standards with the best given additional funding to expand and the worst allocated fewer places or forced to close. Ireland, Sweden, and the Netherlands have all used similar approaches to increase the relevance of teacher training.

Programs of ongoing professional development for teachers based on the same principles have proved similarly successful. Creating opportunities for more effective teachers to coach their colleagues in the classroom has been the essential feature of most reforms that have led to fast improvements in student outcomes.[29] For instance, Boston, England, and Ontario achieved substantial improvements in student outcomes through programs centred on providing good guidance to teachers, one-on-one coaching in classrooms, and providing ways to increase the level of cooperation and collaboration both within and between schools. Through those approaches,

Boston tripled the number of students meeting the states' minimum standards in mathematics – from 25% to 74% – over a period of just six years. England achieved the first substantial improvement in standards of numeracy and literacy in more than 50 years.

Getting the right people to become teachers, developing them well, and constructing a system which provides the challenge, leadership, and freedom to enable them to perform to the best of their potential form the core of an effective school system. The final core element is ensuring that those teachers are deployed to ensure that every child receives a good education.

8.

The Grandmaster Experiment

(Challenging inequity in educational performance)

There is much evidence to support the fundamental belief of many educators that every child is capable of reaching the highest levels of achievement. However, few school systems produce results consistent with that belief. In many, a child's performance at school depends mainly on where they are born, who their parents are, and where they go to school. Yet a range of studies and interventions prove that it is possible to improve equity, reduce the effect of background on student achievement, and increase the system's ability to realize the potential of every child. Providing universal access to high-quality preschool programs, lengthening school days, and constructing a series of interventions to help individual students who are falling behind all improve equity and raise the performance of the system as a whole.

Almost every child is capable of reaching the highest levels of educational achievement

The Hungarian psychologist Laszlo Polgar was born in Budapest in 1946. In the late 1960s he wrote a book called "Bring Up Genius!" in which he set out his theory that "geniuses are made, not born." After studying hundreds of biographies of great thinkers, he had come to the conclusion that, with the right training and perseverance, anybody could reach the highest levels of cognitive performance. In order to test his theory he decided to do an experiment.[1]

After the publication of his book, he and his wife Klara had three daughters – Susan, Sofia, and Judit – born between 1969 and 1976.

Laszlo decided to train them to be great chess players. The choice of chess was somewhat arbitrary: Laszlo says the idea sparked when Susan, his first daughter, was aged four and found a chess set in a cupboard. Years later, Sofia mused about the choice: "If I had invested the same effort and time in tennis as I did in chess, I would have long since been a millionaire. If I had devoted myself to medicine in the same way, maybe I would have won the Nobel Prize." In preparation, all three were taught at home, with an emphasis on mathematics, languages (Laszlo had also decided that they should all be multilingual), and chess, despite the protests of the Hungarian authorities, who thought Laszlo was mad. In the end, however, Laszlo and Klara's program of schooling prevailed, particularly once the first signs emerged that their children were making some extraordinary achievements.

His daughters became three of the best chess players the world has known, a particularly impressive feat in a sport where the top players are almost exclusively male. Judit, the third of the sisters, is currently the top female chess player in the world (she first reached the number one spot at the age of 13), the only woman in the top 100, and by far the most successful female chess player in history. Susan was women's world champion from 1996 to 1999, and ranks after her sister as the second best female player ever. Sofia, the least successful of the three on the chess board, is still ranked 6th in world among female players. Laszlo had planned to later repeat the experiment with three boys adopted from another country in order to prove that the achievement could be repeated with a group of children who were not related to him, though unfortunately for the research community, the later plan was vetoed by his wife.

Laszlo's experiment sits among a growing body of evidence from a range of sources which supports the fundamental belief of many educators that every child has the potential to reach the highest levels of performance. Studies of identical twins separated when young suggest that education and upbringing are far more important than innate characteristics in determining educational success. Studies of highly successful individuals show almost no consistent links to factors other than education, training, and upbringing: "nothing shows that innate factors are a necessary prerequisite for expert-level mastery in most fields. ... Unless you're dealing with a cosmic anomaly like Mozart an enormous amount of hard work is what makes a prodigy's performance look so effortless."[2] The only exception to that rule appears to be a correlation between height and success in some sports, particularly basketball. As Frank Layden, former coach of the Utah Jazz, likes to say, "you can't teach height" (though at 5ft 3, basketball-player Muggsy Bogues proves that nothing is impossible).

Variation in educational performance between different countries also suggests that every child can reach high levels of performance. In Mathematics, half of Singaporean students perform at a level equivalent to the top 10% of students in the United States. That suggests either that Singaporeans are inherently smarter than Americans (unlikely), or that with the right schooling the average American student might also be capable of performing at a level currently achieved by only the top 10% of Americans. Similarly, if most students in the bottom 25% of students in Finland can perform at the same level as the average student in the United States, that suggests that even those students who most school systems cast aside as low performing could reach good levels of achievement with the right support. Unfortunately, few school systems produce outcomes consistent that belief.

In most countries, student background affects achievement more than any other factor

In most school systems, where a child is born and who their parents are influence their chances of succeeding at school more than any other variable. By age ten, the difference in reading levels between children of parents who have been to university, and children of parents who have not completed lower secondary school, is already equivalent to three years of schooling. The further they progress through school, the larger the achievement gap becomes.

Those differences in performance at school in turn influence the chances that a child will graduate or go to university. In the United States as a whole, students from low-income families are six times less likely to go to university than students from professional families.[3] In England students eligible for free school meals, the most widely used proxy for social disadvantage, are less than half as likely to gain five GCSEs including English and Mathematics (the target standard for 16 year olds) as other students, and twice as likely to leave school with no qualifications at all.[4] Children who grow up in care are more likely to go to prison than university. Those patterns

Figure 15: The relationship between background and educational outcomes for students in the OECD

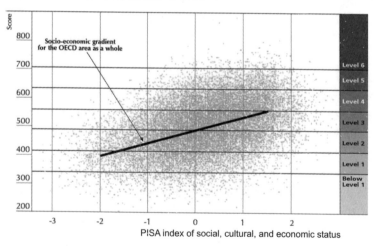

Source: OECD, *PISA 2006,* p. 183

are replicated in almost every country in the world.

The graph opposite shows the relationship between a student's background and their results in the PISA tests for all of the OECD countries. Each point on the graph represents 500 students with similar background and performance. There is a clear correlation between background and performance: the effect of moving from a socioeconomic background one standard deviation below average to a background one standard deviation above average is equivalent to three years of schooling, and almost none of the students scoring at the top level of performance are from the poorest 20% of students in the OECD.

Importantly, the graph also shows that the relationship between a student's background and their performance at school is linear. Every increase in the socioeconomic status of a child's family leads to an equal increase in their performance at school; or in other words, background affects the performance of all students, not just those at the bottom of the socioeconomic ladder. The impact of moving from a low socioeconomic background to an average one is the same as the impact of moving from an average background to a high one. This is important because most of the popular discussion on equity in schools, and many of the policies designed to improve it, are based on the incorrect assumption that the problems of inequity in education are concentrated in the lowest performing schools in the lowest-income areas. In contrast, the data shows that while the effect of background is greatest in the lowest-income areas, background affects student achievement across the socioeconomic spectrum, and by implication, policies to reduce it need to work on improving support for students throughout the school system, not just in those areas with the highest levels of poverty.

The graph also shows that while there is a correlation between a student's background and their performance at school, there is also a lot of variation in the performance of individual students from similar backgrounds. So while background influences results, it does not determine them. More importantly, other data from PISA show that the extent to which background determines educational achievement varies greatly between different schools and different school systems. The effect of student background on performance in the United States is almost double the same effect in Canada. In Iceland, Japan, and Finland, children from disadvantaged backgrounds are two or three times more likely to be low achievers in Mathematics than students from more advantaged backgrounds. In Belgium, they are more than five times more likely to be low achievers. So while background affects performance everywhere, the magnitude of that effect depends greatly on where a child goes to school.

Differences in outcomes are often driven by differences in what happens at home, though the best schools largely compensate for those differences

Differences in achievement between students from different backgrounds arise for a combination of reasons. Children from low-income backgrounds often start school later and are less likely to attend good preschool programs. In many countries they are also likely to go to less effective schools with less effective teachers. However, much of the difference stems from how much they learn when they are not at school. What happens when children are at home, and in particular, what happens when they are very young, has a major effect on how well they do at school.

During the mid-1990s, two researchers at the University of Kansas – Betty Hart and Todd Risley – conducted an extensive investigation into how children from different backgrounds develop and what causes the differences. Over a period of two and a half years they spent one hour every month observing each of 42 different families. 13 of the families were from professional backgrounds, 23 were from working-class backgrounds, and six were families on welfare support. They looked both at how much the children in the families were learning and what in the behaviour of those families might explain the differences. As part of the work, they transcribed and analysed hundreds of hours of conversations recorded in each of the families.

Over the course of the study, they uncovered massive differences in how much the children were learning at an early age. By the age of three, the children of the professional parents already knew twice as many words as the children of the parents on welfare. They had started talking three to four months earlier, but more importantly, they were adding words at a faster rate. The children in the professional families also scored higher on IQ tests. While the three year olds in the welfare families knew 525 words and had an average IQ score of 79, the three year olds in the professional families knew 1,110 words and had an average IQ score of 117.[5]

More strikingly, there were big differences in what was happening in the families, which led the researchers to conclude that the difference in how much the children were learning was less the result of who the parents were, and more the result of what they did. Children in the families on welfare heard half as many words each hour as children in the working-class families, and one third as many words as the children in the professional families. The researchers calculated that by their fourth birthdays, the children in the professional families would have heard around 45 million words, the children in the working-class families 26 million, and the children in the welfare families just 13 million.

There were also differences in the types of language used. Hart and Risley tracked the number of encouragements each child heard compared to the number of prohibitions. In the professional families, children heard six times as many encouragements as prohibitions: an average of 32 encouragements each hour and five prohibitions. In the working class families, the ratio was two-to-one, or twelve encouragements and seven prohibitions each hour. However in the welfare families, the situation was reversed. The children were hearing eleven prohibitions and five encouragements each hour. The discourse in the professional families was also more sophisticated than in the welfare families, with longer discussions, more questions, and more analysis of events and feelings. The study concluded that the children in the professional families were developing faster not only because they heard more words but also because the types of language they were exposed to were more sophisticated and more encouraging. A follow-up study conducted when the children were ten years old found substantial differences in their achievement at school closely correlated with their vocabulary and IQ scores at age three.

These differences in early development have been confirmed by a range of larger studies in other countries. For instance, recent research in the United Kingdom found that by their third birthday children of university graduates are already one year ahead of the children of less educated parents in the development of their vocabulary. Tests of school-readiness, which examine their ability to recognize shapes, letters, numbers, colours, and sizes, place them 13 months ahead of their peers.[6] These differences are even more significant than they might appear at first because early learning has a disproportionately large impact on later educational outcomes.[7]

Moreover, this increased learning at home does not stop when children start attending school. Even when a child is enrolled in full-time education, they will still be spending less than 15% of their time in the classroom. What happens during the other 85% of their time is extremely important, particularly for the development of more generic skills like conversational literacy, problem solving, leadership, or creativity. One long-term study involving extended observation of many families found that "middle-class parents engaged in practices of concerted cultivation. ... They actively fostered and assessed their children's talents opinions and skills. They scheduled their children for activities. They reasoned with them. ... [Conversely, in the working-class families] there was less speech (including less whining) ... boundaries between adults and children were clearly marked; parents generally used language not as an aim in itself but more as a conduit for social life."[8]

Those differences both in what happens before children start school, and in what happens after they leave school each day, constitute a major challenge for those who seek to achieve greater equity in education, and one which is unlikely to ever be fully overcome. However, despite those differences, a range of studies show that good schooling can partly or even entirely compensate for the effects of background on student performance. In fact, one of the major insights from the PISA data is that the average socioeconomic background of the students in the school a child goes to is a more important influence on that child's performance than his or her own background. Children who come from poor backgrounds but go to schools where most children come from more wealthy backgrounds outperform children who come from wealthy backgrounds but go to school with children from poorer backgrounds. Put differently, for the average child in the OECD, which school they go to matters more than who their parents are.[9] KIPP and other successful schools demonstrate that children from poor families can consistently reach the highest levels of achievement. And a few school systems demonstrate that a range of policy approaches can improve equity across the system as a whole.

Good early education is critical to addressing educational inequity
The first step towards increasing equity is to ensure that every child has access to high quality early education. Early education is important not only because it establishes an important foundation for later educational success, but also because it prevents disparities in cog-

nitive development from becoming insurmountably large before children start school. In fact, preschool appears to offer the highest return of any investment in education, partly because good early education itself leads to increased achievement, but perhaps more importantly, because it increases learning during each subsequent year of schooling.[10] Whether or not a child attends preschool has a substantial impact on how much they achieve later in their education, particularly if they come from a disadvantaged background or do not speak the main language of the country they live in at home.[11]

One of the most powerful examples of the impact of preschool education comes from a study conducted in Michigan starting in the 1960s. The original aim of the study was to examine the impact of providing high-quality preschool programs to disadvantaged children. Researchers selected 123 African-American three-year olds to participate in the study. All of the children selected were at a high risk of low achievement in education: they were all from a minority group, they came from poor families or disadvantaged backgrounds, and all of them scored below 85 on an IQ test at the beginning of the study. Many of them were close to the borderline for being classified as having special educational needs. Of the 123 kids in the study, 58 were randomly selected to attend a high-quality two-year preschool program. Students on the program attended preschool for two-and-a-half hours each day, five days a week. On top of that, they were visited by their teacher at home for one-and-half hours each week. During that time, the teachers would provide one-on-one teaching to the kids in their own homes, and would also coach parents on how to help their children to learn. The other 65 children selected for the study received no preschool education – they were a control group. At the end of the two-year study, the students entered the regular education system as equals. Researchers have tracked the two groups of students over the forty years since the study started and in doing so, have built up a striking picture of the impact of early education on future outcomes.

On almost every measure, the lives of the children who attended the preschool program were radically different from the lives of the children who did not attend. They had higher test scores throughout their time at school, and were more likely to graduate from high school. Three times as many met the basic achievement standards at age 14. At age 27, they were earning more, working in better jobs, and almost three times more likely to own their own home. They were four times less likely to have been arrested for dealing drugs. They got married three years earlier, were less likely to divorce, and had fewer children out of marriage. When asked, they said that they had closer and stronger relationships with their friends and families.[12]

Figure 16: Outcomes at age 27 for disadvantaged students who attended a high-quality preschool program (%)

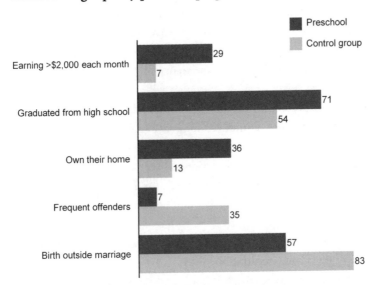

Source: Schweinhart, L., *The High Scope Perry Preschool Study Through Age 40,* 2005

These differences were still as strong a decade later: at age 40, the program participants were earning 42% more than the control group.[13] The kids in the program had just 14 hours of preschooling each week when they were three and four years old, and yet they had completely different lives aged 40 as a result.

Given those benefits, there has been a sustained investment in increasing enrolment in preschool in many countries, particularly over the past decade. Some countries have succeeded in providing high-quality preschool to every child. However, in many, a significant proportion of children, generally from the lowest income groups, do not attend preschool.[14] In the United States only half of children aged three and four are enrolled in preschool programs, and children from low-income families are half as likely to attend preschool as children from high-income families. Where significant numbers of children are not enrolled in preschool programs, that not only reduces the overall effectiveness of the school system, but also increases inequity because children from high-income families who are already ahead at an early age have that advantage reinforced by attendance at preschool, while those who are already behind fall further behind through non-attendance or poor quality programs.

However, even in those countries which do have universal enrolment in preschool, that alone is insufficient to guarantee more equitable outcomes. France has long had full enrolment in its *écoles maternelles* from age three, and yet has some of the highest levels of educational inequity in the developed world.[15] How inequity and underperformance are tackled once children start school appears to be just as important for ensuring equitable outcomes overall.

In general, assigning students with lower performance to separate schools or classes amplifies inequity

By the time students reach school, and in particular, by the time they reach the higher grades of schooling, the gap between the highest and lowest performing students is substantial. For instance, in the United States, the difference between the mathematics scores of the top 10% of 14-year olds and the bottom 10% of 14-year olds is equivalent to eight years of schooling.[16] Broadly speaking, school systems have three options for accommodating that range of performance. First, they can divide students between schools according to their educational performance. In Germany, for instance, most students attend one of three main school types from the age of 10: the *Gymansium* generally takes the highest performing students, the *Realschule* those in the middle, and the *Hauptschule* those at the lowest end of the performance spectrum. Second, schools can divide students into different classes within the same school (streaming) according to ability. In England, for instance, most secondary schools and some primary schools divide students into classes according to ability. Finally, they can support teachers to teach to a wide range of abilities within a single classroom, without dividing according to performance. Finland, among others, uses this model up to age 15.

Intuitively, the first two models appear to be more promising. Grouping students according to their academic ability would allow teachers and schools to pitch teaching and expectations at their level, and reduce the complexity of managing classes with a large range of abilities. Where the differences in performance between students are extremely large, this may be the only way to practically address the needs of all students. Some schools and a few school systems stream students according to their ability, and achieve high performance as a result.

However, in most systems, tracking or streaming students actually increases inequity without producing any improvement in the overall performance of students.[17] In the PISA tests, those school systems which select students into different schools according to ability at an early age also have the highest levels of inequity.[18]

Streaming students within schools has a similar but smaller effect: on average, it leads to a fall in performance of nine points on the PISA tests.[19] In particular, the data show that while the top students generally gain a small benefit from streaming or tracking, students placed into the lower ability groups suffer a larger fall in performance.[20]

That fall occurs for a number of reasons. First, grouping students based on ability rarely produces groups of students with homogenous learning needs. Students with the same average performance will have widely varying strengths, weaknesses, learning styles, and barriers to learning. Moreover, the tests used to divide them into groups are unlikely to be highly accurate measures of either their current performance, or, more importantly, the areas in which they need support to make further progress.[21] These two factors mean that the benefits to teaching and learning from grouping are actually much less than they might appear. At the same time, there are a series of negative effects from grouping which tend to dominate the benefits. When students with lower performance are grouped together, there is a tendency for teachers to accept rather than tackle their lower performance: teachers reduce their expectations of students, avoid complex subjects, and set lower targets for how much progress they expect students to make.[22] More importantly, when students are grouped according to ability teaching tends to be less differentiated and less responsive to their individual needs.[23] One review noted that "the view that grouping pupils by ability ('sets') removes the need to match teaching to their different needs is common."[24] This is compounded by a tendency for schools with lower-performing students to attract less able teachers, and for less effective teachers to be placed with lower ability groups within schools. In England, the schools inspectorate has found that "the highest proportion of inadequate lessons (15%) [is] in sets containing low-attaining pupils in secondary schools,"[25] despite the fact that these are the students most in need of high-quality teaching. Finally, but perhaps most importantly, placing students in schools or classes labelled as low ability is highly damaging to their morale, their expectations of themselves, and their expectations of each other, further contributing to their lower performance. Because all of those effects hit students from the lowest socioeconomic backgrounds hardest they have the additional effect of increasing inequity in the system.

Far more effective than grouping students based on ability is to intervene to help the lowest performing students catch up with their peers. There is a range of interventions which school systems can use to do that. Some are proven to be highly effective at helping individual students to catch up and in raising equity in the system as a whole. However, often the most commonly used interventions are also the least effective.

Interventions to support individuals who are falling behind are the most important means of raising equity, but only if they are the right interventions

Students can fall behind at school for a range of reasons. Sometimes they start school at a lower level of cognitive development than their peers and never make up the difference. Sometimes they lack the support from their parents or home which many other students enjoy. Sometimes there are specific educational blocks – gaps in or barriers to their understanding – which obstruct progress. Difficulties with reading in particular often block learning across a range of subjects. In other cases, the causes are emotional, psychological, or physiological. Whatever their cause, those blocks hinder further learning both because much learning in schools is cumulative and depends on successful mastery of earlier material, and because they destroy confidence and expectations for future learning for the student, and often for their peers and teachers as well. In fact early difficulties in learning are the most common cause of failure at the later stages of schooling. As one superintendent notes, "we know as early as grade three which students may well not complete high school because they have literacy problems."[26]

The best teachers are able to tackle many of those problems on their own during the regular school day. Some experts attribute much of the success of Asian school systems to the fact that their teachers are particularly persistent and effective in this respect; "even in large classes, these teachers go out of their way to make sure that every child is on top of the material."[27] But often, resolving those problems requires more time and expertise than can be delivered within the context of normal classroom teaching alone.

Faced with that challenge, many schools and school systems do very little. Across the OECD as a whole, one quarter of students say that they do not receive extra help from their teachers if they need it.[28] Other school systems intervene but in ways that do little to help students to progress. One of the most common interventions to tackle underperformance in schools is grade repetition. Students who are falling behind the rest of their age group repeat a year of schooling, normally in the same school with the same teachers.[29] Across the OECD as a whole, three to four percent of students are required to repeat a grade each year. In some systems rates of grade repetition are much higher: in France, the developed country with the highest rates of grade repetition, four out of every ten students will have repeated a year by the age of 15.[30]

The main problem with grade repetition is that it does not work. Despite very high rates of repetition, for instance, the performance of the bottom 10% of students in France is among the lowest in the world. Only Italy, who's performance is pulled down by very low rates of achievement in the south of the country, scores worse. Official reports suggest that "*redoublement* has no noticeable effect on a child's progress."[31] Studies in other parts of the developed world consistently show that students who repeat a year "tend to fall further and further behind promoted peers who had very similar achieve-ment profiles in the year prior to grade repetition."[32] At the same time, grade repetition has a range of negative effects on the students involved: it is "stressful … and associated with reduced self-esteem, impaired peer relationships, alienation from school, and sharply in-creased likelihood of eventual dropout."[33]

The fact that grade repetition does not work should not be sur-prising. A student who is held back will generally be among the low-est-performing 10% of students. Put differently, this means that a typical ninth grade student who is held back will be performing at sixth grade level. Clearly, there is something that is blocking their ability to learn. That barrier may be the teacher, the teaching tech-nique, the curriculum, the school, or the other students. It may be a psychological or emotional barrier, or it may come from something happening outside the school. Whatever it is, a barrier exists. Taking that ninth grade student who is performing at sixth grade level and putting them back into the same eighth grade class where they did not learn very much last year, often with the same teacher, the same textbook, the same school … the same everything, does nothing to address that barrier, and as a result, does not tend to produce much change in performance. In fact, their performance gets worse, be-cause the negative effects of grade repetition dominate any positive benefit associated with the additional year of teaching.

That failed intervention comes at a substantial cost. There is cost to the student, who's pre-existing sense of failure and, probably, dis-satisfaction with schooling is compounded by being labelled a fail-ure, being required to repeat an experience which was clearly of little value in the first time, and then finally, discovering that their per-formance is largely unchanged as a result. There is also a significant financial cost, comprising both the cost of providing an extra year of schooling, and also the opportunity cost of the student's time, which is estimated at around $US 20,000 for each student who repeats a grade. Where rates of grade repetition are very high, that financial cost can severely reduce the resources available to ensure that students do not fail in the first place. In some African countries with very high rates of grade repetition, grade repetition has the effect of reducing the overall amount of funding available to every student by as much as one third.

In contrast, a few school systems have developed highly effective systems for intervening to help students who are falling behind. Perhaps the most effective are in Finland. The bottom 10% of students in Finland perform at a higher level than the bottom 10% of students in any other country. By age 15, they are two full years ahead of the bottom 10% of students in France in mathematics and two and a half years ahead in reading. Across the whole of Finland, only around 300 students fail to successfully complete their basic education each year.[34] This equity in outcomes distinguishes Finland from other good school systems. For instance, while the top 10% of students in New Zealand perform at the same level as their Finnish peers, the bottom 10% are a year and a half behind.

Finland achieves those results through a series of staggered early interventions to support students who are falling behind. Classroom teachers are responsible for identifying students who need additional support to keep pace with their peers beyond what can be provided during regular classroom hours. Each school employs "special education" teachers, on average one for every seven to eight classes, who then provide additional instruction to students who need it one-on-one or in a small group. When learning difficulties stem from problems outside of the school, special education teachers are responsible for assembling the necessary team of welfare officers, healthcare providers, social workers, or other professionals to overcome the barrier to learning. Approximately 20% of students receive support in this way every year. Overall, the system of interventions is based on two key principles which distinguish it from interventions in other countries: "intensification, or providing more time by more instructors; and alternative approaches (rather than 'more of the same')."[35]

In some other school systems with large numbers of students from low-income backgrounds, those interventions and focus on helping every student to succeed are complemented by additional learning time. If barriers to learning are not removed, or if teaching is not of a high quality, providing more classroom time is unlikely to lead to more learning. However, even once they are removed, many students, particularly those who have already fallen a long way behind, are unlikely to be able to catch up without additional time at school. KIPP, which has been highly successful in getting students who are performing well below grade level up to high levels of achievement, provides about 60% more time in class than the average school system.

Ensuring that every student receives the support they need to reach the target standard therefore also implies that schools which serve greater numbers of students who are at risk of falling behind will need to receive greater funding than other schools. That additional funding is required both because those students will require more teaching to get to the same standard as other students, and because schools in poorer areas tend to be less attractive to teachers and principals, and therefore need to pay higher salaries in order to attract the same quality of teachers. Though giving those schools more funding will not necessarily lead to greater equity unless that funding is used in the right ways, in the absence of additional funding, it is almost certain that it will not occur at all.

In many countries, schools which serve students in low-income areas are denied that additional funding. In the United States, for instance, schools in low-income areas receive almost $1,000 less funding per student each year than schools in high-income areas.[36] That means that those schools are less able to fund the additional support that the students they serve need, and also that their students are more likely be taught by unqualified or inexperienced teachers.[37] In combination, those two facts mean that schools are likely to amplify rather than reduce inequity in educational outcomes.

In contrast, a few school systems have developed funding formulae which ensure that schools in areas with large numbers of students who are at risk of falling behind receive the additional funding they need. The province of Alberta in Canada funds school districts based on the number of students they enrol and the geographical circumstances of the school. It then adds additional funding based on the number of students with English as a second language, the number of students from native communities, the number of families living below the low-income threshold, the number of years of education completed by mothers of children at the schools, the number of single-parent families, and the student mobility rate. Combined with a strong accountability system, the funding formulae enable schools with larger numbers of at-risk students to attract good staff and fund additional instruction, producing a high level of equity in outcomes as a result.

Inequity in education not only represents a failure of society to give everyone an equal chance in life, it also represents a waste of talent and is a significant driver of a range of social problems from crime to long-term unemployment. Often one of the greatest barriers to tackling equity is the perception that there is a trade-off between equity and performance: that efforts to raise the performance of the lowest-performing students will compromise the performance of the best. In a few cases where countries have implemented reforms to increase equity badly this has indeed been the case. However, in general, that perception is wrong. One insight from international test data is that school systems with high average performance and large numbers of students scoring at the highest levels also tend to have higher levels of equity than other school systems.[38] That makes sense:

school systems which provide everyone with opportunities to learn and support anyone who falls behind make the most of the raw human talent they have, and reach higher overall levels of performance as a result. The most reassuring conclusion supported by the international test data is that trade-offs between equity and performance do not exist; that increasing equity is not only good in and of itself, it is also one of the most effective ways to raise the average performance of the system as a whole.

9.

The Gates of Paradise

(Final thoughts on the art of school reform)

Seven themes, described in the previous chapters, lie at the core of building a successful school system. Very few of the policies described herein are complex; as one friend and experienced educationalist often says, "none of this is rocket science." Yet, many school systems have struggled to achieve even modest improvements in their performance, and many well-designed reforms led by talented and well-intentioned individuals have quickly run into terminal difficulties. Some reforms though have succeeded, and a few school systems have achieved continuous improvement over a long period of time. Their experiences tell us something more about the art of successful school reform.

Sustained attention to detail

In 1401, the *Arte del Calimala* announced a competition to build a set of doors for the Baptistery in Florence. Several of the greatest artists of the Renaissance competed for the commission, but the work was eventually awarded to the 25-year old Lorenzo Ghiberti, who narrowly beat his rival, the 26-year old Filippo Brunelleschi. Following his defeat in the competition, Brunelleschi abandoned sculpture, travelled to Rome to study the ruins of the Roman Empire, turned his attention to architecture, and ultimately went on to design several of the greatest buildings in Florence. Perhaps the greatest was the dome of the Cathedral, a commission he won in another competition with Ghiberti in 1419. In the meantime, Ghiberti worked on his set of doors for the Baptistery for the next 21 years.

He established a workshop to train artists to assist him in the production of the doors: a system of apprenticeship which produced Donatello, Michelozzo, Masolino, and Uccello. He used a new bronze-casting technology to create superior panels. He and the *Arte del Calimala* carefully managed the work over a period of more than two decades. On completion of the doors, he won a further commission to create a second set of doors for the other side of the Baptistery. He worked on this second set of doors, applying the techniques and lessons learned from the first, for the following 27 years. The result was one of the greatest works of the Renaissance: Michelangelo later claimed that the doors were great enough to adorn the entrance to Paradise itself, earning them the epithet, "The Gates of Paradise." The originals were removed from the Baptistery in 1990, and are now housed in the *Galleria Degli Uffizi*, next to the Ponte Vecchio on the banks of the Arno.

Great works of human creativity are often assumed to be the product of genius; spontaneous outpourings of creativity from exceptionally talented individuals. Ghiberti's creation of the Baptistery doors, like so many other works of human ingenuity, demonstrates that even the greatest works of art are as much the product of competitive tendering, performance management, accountability systems, apprenticeship models, and new technologies as they are the product of moments of individual creative genius. More importantly, the *Gates of Paradise* were not the work of a single day or month of frenzied creation, but rather the outcome of almost 50 years of relentless practice, preparation, execution, and precise attention to detail.

The same is true of great school systems. All schools ultimately depend on the talents, drive, inspiration, and creativity of individual teachers to get every child to reach their true potential. Yet whether they enjoy the privilege of having those people is not the product of chance or circumstance, but rather the result of establishing and relentlessly attending to the conditions under which the emergence of such a group of people becomes possible. Those school systems which have improved have done so not through a single year of reform, but rather through long periods of sustained attention to improving the detail of every aspects of the school system. Singapore achieved its current outstanding performance in education through 50 years of continuous improvement. The same is true of Alberta, Hong Kong, Finland, Shanghai, and other school systems with high educational outcomes. As Michael Barber notes in his account of delivering results across British public services: "Stubborn persistence, relentless monotony, attention to detail, and glorying in routine are vastly underestimated in the literature on government and political history. ... [But] the key insight [from our work] is that well-established routines are as important to ... the delivery of results as major decisions on strategy or people."[1]

Yet such sustained and consistent leadership of school systems is rare. In the United States, for instance, the average superintendent in an urban school district stays in position for less than three years.[2] Kansas City has had 25 school superintendents in less than 40 years.[3] Even where leadership is more sustained, priorities change quickly and policies are rarely pursued through to completion. "Local reform initiatives are typically characterized by volatility – jumping nervously from one reform idea to the next over relatively short periods of time – choosing reforms that have little impact on instruction or student learning and implementing them in shallow ways."[4] As Michael Barber notes: "After a while, the hype of another announcement generates no more than a marginally raised eyebrow and a purse of the lips. 'Reforms are like London buses,' one public servant told me in the 1990s: 'it doesn't really matter if you miss one because there'll be another one along in a minute.'"[5]

Often the root of the problem is a fundamental dilemma that while education reform is a long game – both because the process of change takes time, and because it is often decades before the benefits of improved schooling are felt in the economy or society as a whole – it is a game which is played in a political arena which only rewards tangible progress in the short term, and where those who play are immediately held to account for the political or financial costs of any reform. Many school systems which have improved have started by changing their governance arrangements to create more stability in the top leadership ranks and a more consistent focus on delivering real improvement. Without that stability, sustained improvement is unlikely.

Focus, flexibility, and collaboration

In the middle of December 2008, I travelled to Edmonton in Canada, the last trip of the year and the final leg of the journey which produced this book. In Canada, each provincial government is responsible for establishing and managing its own school system; there is no Canadian school system, only those of individual provinces. Edmonton is the capital of the province of Alberta, and Alberta has arguably one of the best school systems in the world. In 2006, the Province scored slightly ahead of Finland in the PISA tests, making it the top-performing school system in the world, a fact little known because PISA results are generally only reported for the country as a whole.

December is possibly not the best time of year to visit Alberta. The temperature during my stay averaged -24°C (-11°F), a temperature at which the air sparkles as tiny specks of ice catch the low light of the winter sun. Having spent the previous week in North Africa, I felt the change even more than usual. Any physical coldness was more than compensated for by the warmth of my Albertan hosts, but even they questioned the timing of my visit in a characteristically polite manner.

Normally I am nervous about attributing the success of a school system to a set of intangibles: culture, philosophy, or a way of doing things. I prefer 'hard' explanations: robust processes for selecting and training teachers, good measurement systems, strong leadership, intelligent funding formulae, and the like. That is not because the former are not important – a wealth of evidence suggests that they are – but rather because those intangibles still need to be backed by good policies and strategies, and because they are often as much a product of a successful school system as an ingredient for building one.

The hard explanations for Alberta's success are all there. It has a history of employing fewer but better teachers: until a recent class size reduction initiative it had one of the highest student-to-teacher ratios in the developed world. It is careful about selecting teachers and has made teaching an attractive profession with good compensation. It sets high standards for achievement and measures them through a balanced and intelligently-designed accountability system that should be a model for school systems all over the world. It invests in excellent professional development, delivered in schools and classrooms, particularly through the innovative school-led and highly successful Alberta Initiative for School Improvement. It funds schools equitably and fairly. The list could go on.

But if I had to explain why Alberta has been so successful, it would come down to a way of working throughout the system which emphasises three things: focus, flexibility, and collaboration. Focus, because to a degree unusual in school systems, everyone is focused on improving student outcomes. It is an organization which truly lives up to its basic guiding principle that "the highest priority of the education system is the success of every student."[6] Flexibility, because wherever possible the system gives schools and teachers choice over how to achieve their goals. Curriculum is flexible; funding is flexible; improvement strategies are flexible. There is very little prescription from the centre, if any. The only thing which is not flexible is the focus on improving student outcomes. Finally, collaboration, because everything is done with the full participation of everyone involved in the school system; in the words of one official, "every time we do something we involve all the stakeholders" (including the unions). Every initiative is a partnership between schools, universities, parents, government, and the community. That culture of collaboration and partnership runs deep, exemplified, for instance, by a tangled web of secondments between different agencies: secondments from schools to district offices, district offices to unions, unions to universities, and universities to schools. It creates the alignment, mutual understanding, and common sense of purpose required to ensure that the system performs well.

Of course, those features are not unique to Alberta. They are characteristics of a few good school systems, and of many other successful organizations outside of education. In his excellent *Leading Change*, John Kotter argues that a similar set of features, among others, are common to all organizations engaged in successful change.[7] However, they are not common in school systems. Many lack a focus on teaching and learning: the terms of reference for the review of schooling which led to New Zealand's landmark 1989 reform, for instance, "did not mention teachers, students, or student learning."[8] Others fail to embrace some of their most important stakeholders, particularly teachers and teacher unions. Of the great many false dichotomies which some people in the education world like to debate, one of the most ridiculous is a raging debate over whether reforms should be 'pro-student' or 'pro-teacher,' as if improving student outcomes necessarily implies having an antagonistic relationship with the teaching profession and anybody who represents them. While conflict is a likely and often necessary companion on any reform journey, school systems which are unable to form good partnerships with all of those actors who determine their success, lack focus on improving student outcomes, or fail to give schools the flexibility to meet the needs of all of their students, are unlikely to go far.

Plagiarism and good management

Sixteen years before my trip to Alberta, in December 1992, the first text message, bearing the words "Merry Christmas," was sent from a personal computer to a mobile phone in England. The following year, the first commercial text messaging service was launched in Sweden, and telephone operators in other countries rapidly followed suit.

At the time, Teach For America was in its third year. The program had already recruited almost 2,000 teachers, and evidence of its impact was beginning to emerge. Though its first years were turbulent, there was strong evidence even by the mid-1990s that it was a highly successful model for getting talented young teachers into the toughest schools.

In 2002, almost ten years later, the first replica of the Teach For America model emerged in London as Teach First. In 2007, the second emerged in Estonia as Noored Kooli. By 2008, a further six programs based on the Teach For America model were being developed.[9]

In 2008, I sent a text message from a mobile phone in a remote part of Mozambique to a friend in China, the cost of which was charged to an account in the United Arab Emirates. SMS services were available in almost every country in the world, were linked together internationally, and were used by just under half of the world's population. In the telecommunications industry, as in almost every other sector of the economy, innovations and lessons learned in business spread quickly to every corner of the globe. Yet, innovations in education rarely seem to move at all. The spread of Teach For America, the work of a small but deeply passionate and talented group of people, is a remarkable exception. Were it not for the fact that Teach For America and its cousins are private organizations it might not have happened at all. Singapore has done some amazing things in education, as has Cuba, Alberta, New Zealand,

and others, but the practices they have developed almost never move across international frontiers, particularly when those innovations concern lessons about how to improve the system.

Often bureaucrats and academics retort that no such potential to learn or transfer practices across systems is possible, because the cultures in which they operate are so different and complex as to render any such learning impossible. One of my favourite examples is the stubborn insistence of American states that each should develop its own standards for what students should learn in subjects such as mathematics, literacy, and science.[10] When pressed on the issue, one North Carolinian policymaker exclaimed to me, in clear frustration at my line of argument, "but, you see, everything is so different in South Carolina."

That failure to a seek out and copy best practice is representative of a broader absence of good management in many school systems. Some lack even the most basic data on their schools: the school systems I visited included one which did not know how many schools it had, and several which maintained no central record of which teachers taught in which schools. That compares to many of the best companies, which collect and use huge amounts of data. Wal-Mart, for instance, owns what is probably the world's largest data warehouse. It can store hundreds of terabytes of data; in 2004, Wal-Mart was storing more than twice as much data as was held on the entire internet. Wal-Mart knows, on an hourly basis, the level of sales of every single product it sells in every single one of its stores. The best school systems also engage in determined feats of measurement. One Canadian superintendent proudly states that "we relentlessly measure everything we do."[11] Singapore spent millions of dollars building a detailed picture of teaching and learning in individual classrooms, and continuously searches the world for models and practices it can adapt and use in its schools. Those systems also know the limitations of that data; in particular, they strive to be evidence-seeking (collecting data and using it to make informed judgments about policy and practice) without being data-driven (using data to drive decision making and accountability in the absence of professional judgment). However, the fact that they know that their data has limitations does not make them doubt the value of collecting and using it wherever possible.

More broadly, the work of Michael Barber and his colleagues at the Delivery Unit in England demonstrates the difference that good management of reforms makes to their success. Over an eight year period, first in education and then across a range of public services, they reformed the way in which the government managed key reforms, massively increasing their rate of success. Their approach consisted of:

- "Establishing and sustaining clear priorities;
- Applying good, clear, simple methods ('deliverology');
- Ensuring that good people were in key positions ...;
- Clarifying and checking the strength of all the links in the delivery chain;
- Building good, plain-speaking, honest relationships ... so that problems could be identified early and, more often than not, rectified;
- Securing good collaboration between departments on crosscutting issues ...; [and]
- Building and maintaining the routines which drive performance."[12]

Many more school systems prove that the absence of such management condemns even the best designed reform to failure; or put differently, that even the best policy or strategy is worth little in the absence of the capacity to successfully implement it.

Education in the 21st century
At the end of a long journey, some images stick in my mind more

clearly than others; be it the descent into the subway in Moscow, the sight of the Western Wall at sunset, the rush of riding through the streets of Kampala on the back of a scooter, or crossing the Sydney Harbour in the early morning mist. One of the clearest is the sight, all over Africa, of children walking.

Along thousands of miles of African roads, every day, millions of children walk to and from school. Sometimes we would drive a hundred miles without a single break in the stream of children walking. Most played or kicked along footballs as they travelled. A few sang. Many wore no shoes. In the most absurd cases, troops of visibly malnourished children walked slowly along the road in pristine school uniforms, reminiscent of a traditional British private school, and no doubt supplied by an aid agency in a noble, but perhaps not desperately helpful, intervention to support education in the developing world. (The amount of money spent on noble but not desperately helpful projects in Africa is alarming; in one poor country with schools in desperate need of reform I found one organization proudly handing out brand new laptops to children living in areas with no electricity. But that is another problem.)

Attendance rates at the schools themselves often exceed 98%. Many children walk miles to school, without fail, every single day. The sad thing is that, in most cases, the schools themselves are awful. In some African countries, teachers spend less than 20% of their day actually teaching in classrooms. Many teachers lack even the most basic understanding of the subjects they teach. If any teaching is happening at all, the quality is likely to be extremely low. School leaders are ineffective at best; corrupt and destructive at worst. National and international tests suggest that only a small proportion of students in these schools, after five or six years of study, master even the most basic numeracy and literacy skills. Yet, in spite of the tragic state of the schools, the hope that education offers, or at least should offer, keeps those children walking back and forth to school, without fail, every single day.

A few schools, generally those led by extremely determined individuals, prove that this does not have to be the case; that even with the limited human and financial resources available, a school can still deliver at least a reasonable education. Moreover, in most of those countries, there are simple and inexpensive things that can be done at the level of the system that would significantly improve the quality of education that those schools can offer. Unfortunately, those are rarely the things which get funded or implemented.

Perhaps it is remarkable enough that those children go to school at all. In the 21st century, for the first time in human history, almost every child in the world will go to school. Nine out of ten children born at the start of the 21st century will attend at least some primary education, and three out of four will complete primary education.[13] That still leaves some way to go, but it means that more children will go to school than ever before.

However, the central challenge of the 21st century, for both developed and developing countries, will be to raise the quality of that education. Merely ensuring that children attend school is not enough: their chances in life depend not on whether they go to school, but rather on the extent to which their schools and teachers provide them with the knowledge, skills, and values they need to be happy and successful in a rapidly changing world. At present, few schools can claim to do that. Most school systems tolerate a level of failure and inefficiency no longer tolerated in any other sector of the economy; if airlines operated with same level of consistency as schools air travel would have long been relegated to the footnotes of history. Many schools, even whole school systems, can fail, and be left failing, for decades.

What makes that challenge exciting though, is that the rewards for those who can conquer it are also bigger than ever before. Carly Fiorina eloquently describes what makes the 21st century unique:

"This is the first century in the history of humankind where we actually can do anything we choose. ... We can travel into space and see the rings around Saturn. We can go to the depths of the ocean and discover lifeforms we never knew existed. We can destroy the planet. We can save the planet. We can produce enough food to feed everybody in the world. We can choose to let people starve. We can do anything we choose."[14] It is a century in which individuals or small groups of individuals can wield extraordinary power; both the power to build a website from a dorm room at Harvard which changes the way people interact with their friends and earns its creator one hundred million dollars, and the power to fly a plane into a building and change the course of history. How well we can educate the next generation will determine both the extent to which that power can be unleashed, and, perhaps more importantly, the purposes for which is used.

That, in turn, should make the 21st century the most exciting time in the history of humankind to be working in education. It is a century in which schools and teachers who inspire and enable young minds give them access to a greater set of opportunities than that offered to any generation which has proceeded them, a century in which the options for creating stimulating and effective schools are more numerous than ever before, and a century in which education will need to constantly adapt and reinvent itself in order to keep pace with the world it seeks to prepare the next generation to enter. Those who work in education shoulder an awesome responsibility: as Aristotle would have counselled, the course of history lies in their hands.

Notes

Foreword

1. Barber, M., Mourshed, M., *How the world's best-performing school systems come out on top. London*, McKinsey, 2007.

2. Levin, B., Glaze, A., Fullan, M., "Results without Rancor or Ranking: Ontario's Success Story," in *Phi Delta Kappan*, December 2008.

3. Cabinet Office, *Excellence and Fairness*, 2008.

Chapter 1

1. OECD, *Literacy in the Information Age*, 2000, pp. 1-11.

2. Schleicher, A., *Why Education is Key for Europe's Success,* Lisbon Council, 2006. OECD analysis shows that a country's research and innovative output is strongly correlated with the number of high-performing students its school system produces. OECD, *PISA 2006*, 2007, p. 51.

3. Wößmann, L., Schütz, G., *Efficiency and Equity in European Education and Training Systems*, 2006.

4. *Why Education is Key for Europe's Success.*

5. OECD, *Education at a Glance*, 2006.

6. Baum, S., Payea, K., *Education Pays*, College Board, 2004.

7. *Literacy in the Information Age*, p. 78.

8. *Literacy in the Information Age*, p. 65.

9. Currie, J., Thomas, D., *Early Test Scores, School Quality, and SES*, 1997.

10. Blanchflower, D., Oswald, A., "Well-being over Time in Britain and the USA," *Journal of Public Economics*, 2005.

11. UNESCO, *Education for All Global Monitoring Report 2005*, 2004, p. 45.

12. Lochner, L., Moretti, E., *The Effect of Education on Crime*, 2003, p. 31.

13. *Education for All Global Monitoring Report 2005*; *Efficiency and Equity in European Education and Training Systems*.

14. UNESCO Institute for Statistics.

15. *No Child Left Behind Act*, 2002.

16. Bishop, J., "Is the Test Score Decline Responsible for Productivity Growth

Decline," *The American Economic Review*, March 1989, pp. 178-197.

17. Rothstein, R., *The Myths and Realities of America's Student Achievement*, Century Foundation, 1998; Iowa Department of Education, *The State Report Card for No Child Left Behind*, 2007.

18. Data on long-term trends are available from several other major tests, however, none are reliable indicators of overall educational performance. The most widely cited are scores on the Scholastic Achievement Test (SAT), which was first administered in a format similar to its current format in 1941. The data shows that average scores on the SAT have declined substantially over time. However, the SAT is not taken by every student in America, and the group of people who do take the test are not representative of the nation as a whole. In particular, since 1941 the number of students taking the test has expanded dramatically. To compare test scores in 1941 with test scores in 2009 is to compare the performance of a small elite group of students taking the test in the 1940s with a much larger and less selective group of students who take the test today; not a reliable comparison of the performance of school system as a whole over time.

19. National Center for Education Statistics, *NAEP 2004: Trends in Academic Progress*, 2005.

20. Education spending per student, after adjusting for inflation, increased by 110%. National Center for Education Statistics.

21. The average student-to-teacher ratio in public schools fell from 22.3 in 1971 to 15.6 in 2004. National Center for Education Statistics.

22. Brooks, G., *Trends in Standards of Numeracy and Literacy in the United Kingdom 1948-1996*, NFER, 1997.

23. Seldon, A., *Blair Unbound*, Simon & Schuster, 2007, p. 107.

24. Statistics Commission, *Measuring Standards in English Primary Schools*, February 2005; House of Commons, *Oral Evidence Taken Before the Children Schools and Families Committee*, 10 December 2007.

25. IEA, *Progress in International Reading Literacy Study 2006 (PIRLS 2006)*, 2007; IEA, *Trends in International Mathematics and Science Survey 2007 (TIMSS 2007)*, 2008.

26. For instance, for Australia see: Rothman, S., *Achievement in Literacy and Numeracy by Australian 14-year olds 1975-1998*, ACER, 2002; IEA, *Trends in International Mathematics and Science Survey 2003 (TIMSS 2003)*, 2004; *PISA 2006*.

27. *Education for All Global Monitoring Report 2005*, p. 60.

28. *Literacy in the Information Age*.

29. Coleman, J., *Equality of Educational Opportunity*, 1966.

30. 43% of the population was illiterate. Seong, D., *Strategic Management of Educational Development in Singapore*, 2006.

31. Goh, C., Gopinathan, S., *The Development of Education in Singapore Since 1965*, 2006.

32. IEA, *Trends in International Mathematics and Science Study 1995 (TIMSS 1995)*, 1996.

33. IEA, *Progress in International Reading Literacy Study 2001 (PIRLS 2001)*, 2002.

34. *TIMSS 2003*; *TIMSS 2007*.

35. *PIRLS 2006*. Though the normal gap between testing cycles is five years, Singapore conducts the tests at different times of the year from other countries to accommodate the different school year (January to November instead of September to July). As a result, the gap between the running of the 2001 and 2006 assessments in Singapore was four years.

36. Spend per primary-school student relative to GDP per capita.

37. As of the school year 2008-2009.

38. Headden, S., "Two Guys ... and a Dream," *US News*, 12 February 2006.

39. www.kipp.org.

40. Matthews, J., "New Teacher Jolts KIPP," *Washington Post*, 19 December 2006.

41. Education Policy Institute, *An Academic Impact Analysis of the Knowledge Is Power Program*, 2005.

42. Sander, W., Rivers, J., *Cumulative and Residual Effects of Teachers on Future Student Academic Achievement*, 1996; Jordan, H., Mendro, R., Weerasinghe, D., *Teacher Effects on Longitudinal Student Achievement*, 1997; Aaronson, D., Barrow, L., Sander, W., *Teachers and Student Achievement in the Chicago Public Schools*, 2003.

43. In mathematics, 55% of variation at the primary level and 53% at the secondary level was attributable to teacher effects. In English, 45% of variation at the primary level and 38% of the variation at the secondary level was attributable to teacher effects. Rowe, K., "The Importance of Teacher Quality," *Issue Analysis No. 22*, 2002, p. 8.

44. "The Importance of Teacher Quality."

45. "New Teacher Jolts KIPP."

46. McBeath, A., *How Edmonton Does It and Why It Works*, 2003.

47. Allington, R., Johnston, P., *What Do We Know About Effective Fourth Grade Teachers*, 2000, p. 2.

48. Barber, M., *Journeys of Discovery*, 2005.

Chapter 2

1. 27% of Californians were born outside the United States, compared to 12% of the population of the United States as a whole.

2. For instance, on a comparison of growth in mathematics scores between the 4th grade and 8th grades, which controls for many contextual effects, California scores 43rd out of 50 states.

3. California Department of Education.

4. Fourth grade reading scores as measured by NAEP.

5. Bohrnstedt, G., Stecher, B. (Eds.), *What We Have Learned About Class Size Reduction in California*, California Department of Education, 2002, pp. 5-6.

6. *What We Have Learned About Class Size Reduction in California*, p. 6.

7. OECD, *Education at a Glance 2000-2007*; National Center for Education Statistics.

8. Ehrenberg, R., Brewer, D., Gamoran, A., Willms, D., "Does Class Size Matter," *Scientific American*, November 2001.

9. OECD, *Attracting, Developing, and Retaining Effective Teachers*, 2005, p. 61.

10. The three states reduced their student-to-teacher ratios by 24%, 23%, and 25% respectively.

11. Reading scores on NAEP showed no improvement; mathematics scores improved but at a slower rate than the national average. *Analysis of data from NAEP and NCES*.

12. Hays, C., "What Wal-Mart Knows About Customers' Habits," *New York Times*, 14 November 2004.

13. The number varied over the course of the experiment.

14. Hanushek, E., "Some Findings from an Independent Investigation of the Tennessee STAR Experiment and from Other Investigations of Class Size Effects," *Educational Evaluation and Policy Analysis 21*, 1999, p. 154.

15. Shapson, S., Wright, E., Eason, G., Fitzgerald, J., "An Experimental Study on the Effects of Class Size," *American Educational Research Journal*, 1980, pp. 141-152.

16. Buckingham, J., "Reflections on Class Size and Teacher Quality," *Issue Analysis 29a*, 2003.

17. Blatchford, P., Basset, P., Brown, P., Martin, C., Russell, A., *The Effects of Class Size on Attainment and Classroom Processes in English Primary Schools*, Institute of Education, 2004.

18. IEA, *Progress in International Reading Literacy Study 2006*, 2007.

19. In 2002, voters in Florida passed a constitutional amendment requiring that

the State reduce class sizes to no more than 18 students in kindergarten through to grade three, no more than 22 students in grades four through eight, and no more than 25 students in high school. The amendment made no provision for funding to cover the cost of the class size reduction, estimated at three billion dollars each year.

20. *What We Have Learned About Class Size Reduction in California*, p. 6.

21. Santiago, P., "The Labour Market for Teachers," in Johnes, G., Johnes, J. (Eds.), *International Handbook on the Economics of Education*, Edward Elgar, 2004, p. 538.

22. Michaelowa, K., Wechtler, A., *The Cost-Effectiveness of Inputs in Primary Education: Insights from the Literature and Recent Student Surveys for Sub-Saharan Africa*, 2006, p. 9.

23. Developing countries are excluded from this analysis. These countries often have large class sizes but low levels of achievement, in general, because they are starting from much lower overall levels of education and development.

24. For instance, between 1975 and 2000, teacher salaries relative to GDP per capita in the developing world fell by an average of 44%, while class sizes decreased overall. *Education For All Monitoring Report 2005*, p. 165.

Chapter 3

1. Only Iceland and Japan have a significantly weaker relationship between socioeconomic status and student performance, though Canada, South Korea, and Norway (but not Sweden or Denmark) have similar equity levels to Finland.

2. Välijärvi, J., Linnakylä, P., Kupari, P., Reinikainen, P., Arffman, I., *The Finnish Success in PISA - And Some Reasons for It*, OECD, 2003.

3. Schleicher, A., *Learning For Tomorrow's World: Results From PISA 2003*, 2005.

4. *The Finnish Success in PISA - And Some Reasons for It*, p. 3.

5. Hopkins, D., *Every School a Great School*, McGraw Hill, 2007, p. 31.

6. Linnakylä, P., Välijärvi, J., *Finnish Students' Performance in PISA*, 2003, p. 4.

7. Ministry of Education (Finland), *Improving School Leadership*, 2007, p. 17.

8. TIMSS and PIRLS, run by the International Association for the Evaluation of Educational Achievement.

9. Hutchings, M., Maylor, U., Mendick, H., Menter, I., Smart, S., *An Evaluation of Innovative Approaches to Teacher Training on the Teach First*

Programme, Institute for Policy Studies in Education, 2006, p. 11.

10. Times, *Top 100 Graduate Employers*, 2007. (Survey undertaken prior to the economic downturn of 2008/2009; both Teach First and Teach For America have seen a further rise in applications as the job market tightens.)

11. Kopp, W., *One Day All Children*, Public Affairs, 2001, p. 7.

12. *Business Week*, "Teach For America Taps Titans," 13 September 2007.

13. *An Evaluation of Innovative Approaches; One Day All Children*.

14. Ofsted, *Rising to the Challenge: A Review of the Teach First Initial Teacher Training Program*, 2008.

15. Decker, P., Mayer, D., Glazerman, S., *The Effects of Teach For America: Findings From A National Evaluation*, 2004; Kane, T., Rockoff, J., Steiger, D., *What Does Certification Tell Us About Teacher Effectiveness*, 2006; *One Day All Children*, p. 99.

16. "Teach For America Taps Titans."

17. Teach For America, "Teach For America Launches Teach For All to Support Development of Its Model in Other Countries," Press Release, 27 September 2007.

18. For a summary of the evidence: see NCTQ, *Increasing the Odds*, 2004; Allington, R., Johnston, P., *What Do We Know About Effective Fourth Grade Teachers*, 2000.

19. Leithwood, K., Day, C., Sammons, P., Harris, A., Hopkins, D., *Seven Strong Claims About Successful School Leadership*, NCSL, 2006; National Audit Office, *Improving Poorly Performing Schools in England*, 2006.

20. Sander, W., Rivers, J., *Cumulative and Residual Effects of Teachers on Future Student Academic Achievement*, 1996; Jordan, H., Mendro, R., Weerasinghe, D., *Teacher Effects on Longitudinal Student Achievement*, 1997; Aaronson, D., Barrow, L., Sander, W., *Teachers and Student Achievement in the Chicago Public Schools*, 2003.

21. Andreas Schleicher, quoted in *Oral Evidence Taken before the Children, Schools and Families Committee*, 10 December 2007.

22. UCAS Statistical Services.

23. Arlosoroff, M., "Math 101 for Teachers," *Haaretz*, 16 April 2007.

24. OECD, *Attracting, Developing, and Retaining Effective Teachers*, 2005, p. 82.

25. Acedo, C., *Teacher Supply and Demand in the Philippines*, 1999, pp. 4-5.

26. *An Evaluation of Innovative Approaches*, p. 14.

27. Relative to the overall size of their school system.

28. *Attracting, Developing, and Retaining Effective Teachers*, p. 53.

29. Barber, M., Mourshed, M., Whelan, F., "Improving Education in the Gulf," *McKinsey Quarterly*, 2007, p. 44.

30. *Increasing the Odds*, p. 8.

31. *Increasing the Odds*, p. 7.

32. Goldhaber, D., Brewer, D., "Does Teacher Certification Matter? High School Teacher Certification Status and Student Achievement," *Educational Evaluation and Policy Analysis, Vol. 22, No. 2*, 2000.

33. *Increasing the Odds*, p. 5; Angrist, J., Guryan, J., *Does Teacher Testing Raise Teacher Quality*, 2005; Bohrnstedt, G., Stecher, B. (Eds.), *What We Have Learned About Class Size Reduction in California*, California Department of Education, 2002. *What does Certification Tell Us About Teacher Effectiveness.*

34. Kim, E., and Han, Y., *Attracting, Developing, and Retaining Effective Teachers: Background Report for South Korea*, 2002, p. xi.

35. *Increasing the Odds*, p.10.

36. *One Day all Children*, pp. 34-5.

37. *Attracting, Developing, and Retaining Effective Teachers*, p. 40.

38. College Board, *Total Group Profile*, 2007, p. 13.

39. For instance, American studies have found that students are less likely to choose to study for a teaching certificate in states where course requirements are larger. Hanushek, E., Pace, R., *Who Chooses to Teach and Why*, 1995.

40. Buckingham, J., "Good Teachers Where They Are Needed," *Issue Analysis 64*, 2005.

41. *An Evaluation of Innovative Approaches*, p. 1.

42. DCSF, *School Workforce in England: Additional Information 8*.

43. "Good Teachers Where They Are Needed," p. 10.

44. For instance the work of Dolton, Hanushek, Manski, Murnane, Olson, and Santiago.

45. Interviews.

46. Milanowski, A., "An Exploration of the Pay Levels Needed to Attract Students with Mathematics, Science, and Technology Skills to a Career in K-12 Teaching," *Education Policy Analysis Archives*, 2003.

47. Hanushek, E., Rivkin, S., *How to Improve the Supply of High Quality Teachers*, 2003, p. 5; Stinebrickner referenced in Santiago, P., "The Labour Market for Teachers."

48. For instance, *How to Improve the Supply of High Quality Teachers*.

49. The variance explained falls to 15% when South Korea is removed from the dataset; including South Korea is justified because it is the strongest example

of the fact that higher salaries contribute to high overall performance. *PISA 2006*. OECD, *Education at a Glance*, 2006.

50. TDA, *Performance Profiles Aggregate Dataset*, 2007.

51. Eurydice, *Education in Europe 2005*, p. 230. *Attracting, Developing, and Retaining Effective Teachers*.

52. *Attracting, Developing, and Retaining Effective Teachers*, p. 43.

53. Ministry of Education (Finland), *Attracting, Developing, and Retaining Effective Teachers: Country Background Report for Finland*, 2003, p. 6.

54. Relative to their GDP per capita.

55. *Attracting, Developing, and Retaining Effective Teachers*, p. 150.

56. Training and Development Agency for Schools (11 August 2005).

Chapter 4

1. HMI, *Ten Good Schools*, 1977, p. 36.

2. Leithwood, K., Day, C., Sammons, P., Harris, A., Hopkins, D., *Seven Strong Claims About Successful School Leadership*, NCSL, 2006, p. 12.

3. Peters, T., Waterman, R., *In Search of Excellence*, Profile, 2003, p. 239.

4. Waters, J., Marzano, R., McNulty, B., *Balanced Leadership*, 2006, p. 5.

5. For instance, Bal, J., De Jong, J., *Improving School Leadership: Background Report for the Netherlands*, OECD, 2007, p. 38.

6. Interviews.

7. *Seven Strong Claims*, p. 4. Leithwood, K., Day, C., Sammons, P., Harris, A., Hopkins, D., *Successful School Leadership: What it is and How it Influences Pupil Learning*, 2008.

8. National Audit Office, *Improving Poorly Performing Schools in England*, 2006, p. 36.

9. Price Waterhouse Coopers, *An Independent Study into School Leadership*, 2007, p. v.

10. *Seven Strong Claims*, p. 8.

11. Bolam, R., Dunning, G., Karstanje, P., *New Heads in the New Europe*, 2000.

12. Leschly, S., *New Leaders for New Schools*, HBS, 2002, p. 6.

13. LeTendre, B., Roberts, B., *A National View of Certification of School Principals*, 2005, p. 10.

14. *A National View of Certification of School Principals*, p. 17.

15. *Seven Strong Claims*, p. 14.

16. *Successful School Leadership*, p. 67.

17. *Successful School Leadership*, p. 69.

18. *Seven Strong Claims*, p. 14.

19. For instance, see OECD, *Improving School leadership*, 2008, pp. 183-186.

20. *Improving School leadership*, p. 169.

21. Ministry of Education (New Zealand), *Improving School Leadership*, 2007, p. 50; Fiske, E., Ladd, L., *When Schools Compete*, Brookings Institution, 2000, p. 90.

22. *Improving School leadership*, p. 158.

23. *Improving School leadership*, p. 161.

24. Interviews.

25. *Background Report for the Netherlands*, p. 66; interviews.

26. *Improving School leadership*, p. 166.

27. Leschly, S., *The Gates Foundation and Small High Schools*, HBS, 2003, p. 7.

28. *PISA 2003*, p. 259.

29. Businessweek, "Bill Gates Gets Schooled," 26 June 2006, p. 67.

30. "Bill Gates Gets Schooled," pp. 65-66.

31. Bernstein, L., Millsap, M., Schimmenti, J., Page, L., Abt Associates, *Implementation Study of Smaller Learning Communities*, Department of Education, 2008.

32. NCSL, *Hard Federations of Small Primary Schools*, 2008, p.3.

33. Interviews.

34. *PISA 2006*.

35. Interviews.

36. *PIRLS 2006*.

37. Schütz, G., West, M., Wößmann, L., *School Accountability, Autonomy, Choice, and the Equity of Student Achievement: International Evidence from PISA 2003*, OECD, 2007, p. 10.

38. Interviews.

39. Boston Public Schools, *The Six Essentials*, 2004.

40. Tee, N., "The Singapore School and the School Excellence Model," *Educational Research for Policy and Practice 2*, 2003, p. 28.

41. Ofsted, Inspection Report, 2002.

42. Ofsted, Inspection Report, 2007.

43. *Improving Poorly Performing Schools in England*, pp. 6-7.

Chapter 5

1. The city of Fiume, where Csikszentmihalyi was born, is now called Rijeka. Though part of Italy when he was born, it became part of Yugoslavia under the Treaty of Paris on the 10th of February 1947, and is now the main seaport of Croatia.

2. Csikszentmihalyi, M., *Flow: The Psychology of Optimal Experience*, Harper Perennial, 1990.

3. Csikszentmihalyi, M., *Good Business: Leadership, Flow and the Making of Meaning*, Penguin, 2003.

4. Marzano, R., *A New Era of School Reform: Going Where the Research Takes Us*, 2000.

5. Peters, T., Waterman, R., *In Search of Excellence*, Profile, 2003, pp. 238-240.

6. UNESCO, *Education for All Global Monitoring Report 2008*, 2007, p. 69.

7. Raymond, M., Hanushek, E., "High Stakes Research" in *Education Next*, 2003; Hanushek, E., Raymond, M., *Does School Accountability Lead to Improved Student Performance*, 2004.

8. Schütz, G., West, M., Wößmann, L., *School Accountability, Autonomy, Choice, and the Equity of Student Achievement: International Evidence from PISA 2003*, OECD, 2007; Fuchs, T., Wößmann, L., *What Accounts for International Differences in Student Performance*, 2004.

9. Álvarez, J., Moreno, V., Patrinos, H., *Institutional Effects as Determinants of Learning Outcomes: Exploring State Variations in Mexico*, 2007.

10. Matthews, P., Sammons, P., *Improvement Through Inspection*, 2004.

11. Michaelowa, K., Wechtler, A., *The Cost-Effectiveness of Inputs in Primary Education: Insights from the Literature and Recent Student Surveys for Sub-Saharan Africa*, 2006, pp. 37-38.

12. *In Search of Excellence*, p. 59.

13. *A New Era of School Reform*, p. 18.

14. Fordham, *The State of State Standards*, 2006, p. 38.

15. Converting standards to a single scale in this way is not a highly precise process, because there are lots of different dimensions to the standards. One

standard might be tougher than another in geometry but less challenging in algebra, or contain less material but at a more challenging level, and so a simple comparison on a single scale masks some of those more subtle differences. It does, nonetheless give us a good overall picture of how the standards compare.

16. Importantly, while there is a relationship between how tough the examinations are and how much progress students make, there is no relationship between how tough the examinations are and the level at which students actually perform. This makes it reasonable to infer that the relationship between the progress students make and the expectations states set is the result of higher expectations leading to better performance, not better performance causing states to set higher standards.

17. *The State of State Standards*, p. 33.

18. *Improvement Through Inspection*, p. 21.

19. *Improvement Through Inspection*, p. 21.

20. Fullan, M., *The Six Secrets of Change*, Jossey-Bass, 2008.

21. National Audit Office, *Improving Poorly Performing Schools in England*, 2006, p. 25.

22. Schleicher, A., *Results from PISA 2003*, 2005.

23. *Improvement Through Inspection*, p. 41.

24. *Does School Accountability Lead to Improved Student Performance*.

25. Commission on No Child Left Behind, *Beyond NCLB*, 2007, pp. 61-2.

26. *Report of the Committee of Council of Education 1864-5*, in Dunford, J., *Her Majesty's Inspectorate of Schools Since 1944*, Woburn, 1998, p. 9.

27. *Beyond NCLB*, p. 62.

28. Interviews; *PISA 2006*, p. 100.

29. Ofsted inspection judgements, primary schools, Autumn 2007 and Spring 2008.

30. Olson, L., "State Test Programs Mushroom as NCLB Mandate Kicks In," *Education Week*, 30 November 2006, p. 11.

31. Greene, J., Winters, M., Forster, G., *Testing High-Stakes Tests: Can We Believe the Results of Accountability Tests? (Civic Report No. 33)*, 2003.

32. *Her Majesty's Inspectorate of Schools Since 1944*, p. 13.

33. *Improvement Through Inspection*, pp. 84-85.

34. *Improvement Through Inspection*, p. 28.

35. *Her Majesty's Inspectorate of Schools Since 1944*, p. 3.

36. Barber, M., *Instruction to Deliver*, Politico's, 2007, p. 314.

37. Often however, the Minister of Education is also the Minister responsible for the Education Review Office.

38. Bill Gates, Interview, 13 November 2006.

39. Podgursky, M., Springer, M., *Teacher Performance Pay*, 2006, p. 3.

40. "The Labour Market for Teachers," p. 542.

41. Rosenthal, M., et al., *Early Experience with Pay-For-Performance from Concept to Practice*, April 2005

42. Beer, M., Cannon, M., *Promise and Peril in Implementing Pay for Performance*, 2004.

43. *Promise and Peril in Implementing Pay for Performance*.

44. Basu, K., "Combating India's Truant Teachers," *BBC*, 29 November 2004.

45. Winkler, D., *The Efficiency of Public Education in Uganda*, World Bank, 2007; Taylor, N., "What's Wrong With South African Schools," *JET Education Conference*, 2008.

46. Cheney, G., Ruzzi, B., Muralidharan, K., *A Profile of the Indian Education System*, 2005, p. 10.

47. World Bank, "Getting Teachers and Doctors to Report to Work," 23 March 2006.

Chapter 6

1. Peters, T., Waterman, R., *In Search of Excellence*, Profile, 2003, p. 4.

2. For instance, see: Eurydice, *Education in Europe*, 2005, B.27 (Employment of teachers) or B.23 (Appointment of School Head).

3. Eurydice; press search.

4. *In Search of Excellence*, p. 65.

5. Schütz, G., West, M., Wößmann, L., *School Accountability, Autonomy, Choice, and the Equity of Student Achievement: International Evidence from PISA 2003*, OECD, 2007.

6. McBeath, A., *How Edmonton Does It and Why It Works*, 2003, p. 17.

7. Liker, J., *The Toyota Way*, McGraw Hill, 1994.

8. Fiske, E., Ladd, L., *When Schools Compete*, Brookings Institution, 2000, pp. 31-32.

9. Perris, L., *Implementing Education Reforms in New Zealand: 1987-1997*, 1998, p. 6.

10. *Implementing Education Reforms in New Zealand*, p. 16.

11. *When Schools Compete*, p. 3.

12. *When Schools Compete*, p. 8.

13. *Implementing Education Reforms in New Zealand*, p. 24.

14. Cross City Campaign for Urban School Reform, *A Delicate Balance: District Policies and Classroom Practice*, 2005, p. 4.

15. Earl, L., Watson, N., Katz, S., *Large Scale Education Reform: Lifecycles and Implications for Sustainability*, CfBT, 2003, p. 9.

16. NAEP, *America's Charter Schools: Results from the NAEP 2003 Pilot Study*, 2004. NAEP, *A Closer Look At Charter Schools Using Hierarchical Linear Modelling*, 2006.

17. *Los Angeles Times*, "Few Parents Move Their Children Out of Failing Schools," 8 November 2004.

18. *Beyond NCLB*, p. 82.

19. Barber, M., *The Learning Game*, Victor Gollancz, 1996, p. 102.

20. See parental responses on the PISA questionnaire. *PISA 2006*, p. 235.

21. *The Learning Game*.

22. *When Schools Compete*, pp. 189-192.

23. *When Schools Compete*, p. 9.

24. Wylie, C., Mitchell, L., *Sustaining Development in a Decentralized System: Lessons from New Zealand*, 2003 p. 3.

25. *When Schools Compete*, p. 9.

26. *When Schools Compete*, p. 9.

27. Interviews.

28. Cowen, N., *Swedish Lessons*, Civitas, 2008.

Chapter 7

1. Garvin, D., "Building a Learning Organization" in Harvard Business School, *Harvard Business Review on Knowledge Management*, HBS Press, 1998, p. 47.

2. Barber, M., *Journeys of Discovery*, 2005.

3. Ofsted, *Mathematics: Understanding the Score*, 2008, p. 12.

4. Schwille, J., Dembélé, M., *Global Perspectives on Teacher Learning:*

Improving Policy and Practice, UNESCO, 2007, pp. 37-8.

5. Hanushek, E., Pace, R., *Who Chooses to Teach and Why*, 1995.

6. Education Review Office, *The Quality of Year 2 Beginning Teachers*, 2004.

7. *Global Perspectives on Teacher Learning*, p. 97.

8. Stannard, J., Huxford, L., *The Literacy Game: The Story of the National Literacy Strategy*, Routledge, 2007.

9. Elmore, R., *School Reform from the Inside Out*, Harvard Education Press, 2006, p. 100; Fullan, M., Hill, P., Crévola, C., *Breakthrough*, Corwin Press, 2006.

10. *School Reform from the Inside Out*, p. 89.

11. Darling-Hammond, L., Bransford, J. (Eds.), *Preparing Teachers for a Changing World*, Jossey-Bass, 2005, p. 409.

12. *Global Perspectives on Teacher Learning*, p. 60.

13. NCTQ, *What Education Schools Aren't Teaching*, 2006, p. 9.

14. Kennedy, A., Mullis, I., Martin, M., Throng, K., *PIRLS 2006 Encyclopaedia: A Guide to Reading Education in the Forty PIRLS 2006 Countries*, IEA, 2007, p. 225.

15. Moyer, D., "Training Daze," *Harvard Business Review*, October 2008, p. 144.

16. Nonaka, I., "The Knowledge-Creating Company" in *Harvard Business Review on Knowledge Management*, p. 28.

17. NCTQ, *Increasing the Odds*, 2004, p. 2.

18. When asked, 60% of teachers in the OECD said they had received no professional development in the last three years. *PISA 2000.*

19. OECD, *Attracting, Developing, and Retaining Effective Teachers*, 2005, p. 22.

20. McBeath, A., *Getting Districtwide Results*, 2006.

21. Hartocollis, A., "Who Needs Education Schools," *New York Times*, 31 July 2005.

22. *Global Perspectives on Teacher Learning*, p. 33.

23. Ramsey, G., *Quality Matters*, 2000, p. 158.

24. Official inquiry, in Buckingham, J., "Good Teachers Where They Are Needed," *Issue Analysis 64*, 2005, p. 3.

25. Britton, E., Paine, L., Pimm, D., Raizen, S., *Comprehensive Teacher Induction: Systems for Early Career Learning*, Kluwer, 2003, p. 31.

26. Fullan, M., *The Six Secrets of Change*, Jossey-Bass, 2008.

27. Latin American Educational Quality Assessment Laboratory, *First International Comparative Study of Language, Mathematics, and Associated*

Factors in the Third and Fourth Grades, UNESCO, 1998, p. 12.

28. Gasperini, L., *The Cuban Education System: Lessons and Dilemmas*, 1999, p. 7.

29. Rand, *Partners in Pittsburg Public Schools' Excellence for All Initiative*, 2007; *The Literacy Game: The Story of the National Literacy Strategy*; Fullan, M., *Professional Development is not Professional Learning*, 2007.

Chapter 8

1. Flora, C., "The Grandmaster Experiment," *Psychology Today*, July 2005; *Economist*, "Who Wants to be a Genius," 11 Jan 2001; *Economist*, "Gifted Children," 8 February 2007; Shvidler, E., "All the Right Moves," *Haaretz*; *Telegraph*, "Queen Takes All," 16 January 2002.

2. Anders Ericsson, quoted in "The Grandmaster Experiment."

3. Swanson, C., *Who Graduates?*, Urban Institute, 2003 (data is for 2001).

4. National Statistics, *Social Trends*, 2007, 3.13.

5. Hart, B., Risley, T., "The 30 Million Word Gap by Age 3," *American Educator*, 2003.

6. Centre for Longitudinal Studies, *Disadvantaged Children Up to a Year Behind by the Age of Three*, June 2007.

7. Cunha, F., Heckman, J., Lochner, L., Masterov, D., *Interpreting the Evidence on Life Cycle Skill Formation*, 2005.

8. Lareau, A., *Unequal Childhoods: Class, Race, and Family Life*, University of California Press, 2003, pp. 238-9.

9. *PISA* 2006, pp. 193-5.

10. Wößmann, L., Schütz, G., *Efficiency and Equity in European Education and Training Systems*, 2006, pp. 10-11.

11. OECD, *Starting Strong II: Early Childhood Education and Care*, 2006, pp. 249-257; Sylva, K., Melhuish, E., Sammons, P., Siraj-Blatchford, I., Taggart, B., Eliot, K., *The Effective Provision of Pre-School Education Project: Findings from the Preschool Period*, 2003.

12. Parks, G., *The High Scope Perry Preschool Project*, 2000.

13. Schweinhart, L., *The High Scope Perry Preschool Study Through Age 40*, 2005.

14. OECD, *Education at a Glance*, 2007, p. 291.

15. *PISA 2006*.

16. *NAEP 2007.*

17. Hanushek, E., Wößmann, L., *Does Educational Tracking Affect Performance and Inequality? Differences-in-Differences Evidence across Countries*, 2005.

18. Schütz, G., West, M., Wößmann, L., *School Accountability, Autonomy, Choice, and the Equity of Student Achievement: International Evidence from PISA 2003*, OECD, 2007, p. 11.

19. *PISA 2003*, p. 258.

20. *School Accountability, Autonomy, Choice, and the Equity of Student Achievement*, p. 33.

21. Vygotsky, L., *Mind in Society* edited by Cole, M., (et al.), Harvard, 1978, pp. 79-91.

22. Ofsted, *Mathematics: Understanding the Score*, 2008, p. 17.

23. *PISA 2003*, p. 264.

24. *Mathematics: Understanding the Score*, p. 48.

25. *Mathematics: Understanding the Score*, p. 17.

26. McBeath, A., *How Edmonton Does It and Why It Works*, 2003, p. 29.

27. Interviews.

28. *PISA 2003*.

29. Brophy, J., *Grade Repetition,* IAE, 2006, p. 12.

30. *Economist*, "Bac to School," 6 September 2007.

31. "Bac to School."

32. *Grade Repetition,* p. 15.

33. *Grade Repetition,* p. 16.

34. Grubb, N., *Equity in Education Thematic Review: Finland*, 2005, p. 22

35. *Equity in Education Thematic Review: Finland*, p. 20.

36. US$868 in 2002. Haycock, K., *The Closing the Achievement Gap*, 2006, p. 52.

37. *The Closing the Achievement Gap*, pp. 59-60.

38. *PISA 2006*, p. 190.

Chapter 9

1. Barber, M., *Instruction to Deliver*, Politico's, 2007, p. 111.

2. Elmore, R., *School Reform from the Inside Out*, Harvard Education Press,

2006, p. 2.

3. Talyor, B., "Urban Superintendents Hard to Keep," *USA Today*, 30 September 2008.

4. *School Reform from the Inside Out*, p. 2.

5. *Instruction to Deliver*, p. 72.

6. Ministry of Education (Alberta), *Principles*.

7. Kotter, J., *Leading Change*, Harvard Business School Press, 1996.

8. Perris, L., *Implementing Education Reforms in New Zealand: 1987-1997*, 1998, p. 6.

9. Teach For All, global website.

10. Fordham, *The State of State Standards*, 2006, p. 12.

11. McBeath, A., *How Edmonton Does it and Why it Works*, 2003.

12. *Instruction to Deliver*, pp. 282-3.

13. UNESCO, *Children Out of School: Measuring Exclusion from Primary Education*, 2005.

14. Fiorina, C., *Leadership and Choice*, 2 May 2007 (lecture).

Bibliography

Aaronson, D., Barrow, L., Sander, W., *Teachers and Student Achievement in the Chicago Public Schools*, 2003.

Acedo, C., *Teacher Supply and Demand in the Philippines*, 1999.

Allington, R., Johnston, P., *What Do We Know About Effective Fourth Grade Teachers*, 2000.

Álvarez, J., Moreno, V., Patrinos, H., *Institutional Effects as Determinants of Learning Outcomes: Exploring State Variations in Mexico*, 2007.

Angrist, J., Guryan, J., *Does Teacher Testing Raise Teacher Quality*, 2005.

Arlosoroff, M., "Math 101 for Teachers," *Haaretz*, 16 April 2007.

The Aspen Institute and the Annenberg Institute, *Strong Foundation, Evolving Challenges*, 2006.

Bal, J., De Jong, J., *Improving School Leadership: Background Report for the Netherlands*, OECD, 2007.

Barber, M., *Delivering Results: The Theory and Practice of Whole System Reform*, 2006.

Barber, M., *Instruction to Deliver*, Politico's, 2007.

Barber, M., *Journeys of Discovery*, 2005.

Barber, M., *The Learning Game*, Victor Gollancz, 1996.

Barber, M., Fullan, M., *Tri-Level Development: It's the System*, March 2005.

Barber, M., Mourshed, M., Whelan, F., "Improving Education in the Gulf," *McKinsey Quarterly*, 2007.

Baum, S., Payea, K., *Education Pays*, College Board, 2004.

Beer, M., Cannon, M., *Promise and Peril in Implementing Pay for Performance*, 2004.

Bernstein, L., Millsap, M., Schimmenti, J., Page, L., Abt Associates, *Implementation Study of Smaller Learning Communities*, Department of Education, 2008.

Bishop, J., "Is the Test Score Decline Responsible for Productivity Growth Decline," *The American Economic Review*, March 1989, pp. 178-197.

Blanchflower, D., Oswald, A., "Well-being over Time in Britain and the USA," *Journal of Public Economics*, 2005.

Blatchford, P., Basset, P., Brown, P., Martin, C., Russell, A., *The Effects of Class Size on Attainment and Classroom Processes in English Primary Schools*, Institute of Education, 2004.

Bohrnstedt, G., Stecher, B. (Eds.), *What We Have Learned About Class Size Reduction in California*, California Department of Education, 2002.

Bolam, R., Dunning, G., Karstanje, P., *New Heads in the New Europe*, 2000.

Boston Public Schools, *The Six Essentials*, 2004.

Britton, E., Paine, L., Pimm, D., Raizen, S., *Comprehensive Teacher Induction: Systems for Early Career Learning*, Kluwer, 2003.

Brooks, G., *Trends in Standards of Numeracy and Literacy in the United Kingdom 1948-1996*, NFER, 1997.

Brophy, J., *Grade Repetition*, IAE, 2006.

Buckingham, J., "Good Teachers Where They Are Needed," *Issue Analysis 64*, 2005.

Buckingham, J., "Reflections on Class Size and Teacher Quality," *Issue Analysis 29a*, 2003.

Business Week, "Bill Gates Gets Schooled," 26 June 2006.

Business Week, "Teach For America Taps Titans," 13 September 2007.

Carnoy, M., *Education for All and the Quality of Education: A Reanalysis*, UNESCO, 2004.

Centre for Longitudinal Studies, *Disadvantaged Children Up to a Year Behind by the Age of Three*, June 2007.

Cheney, G., Ruzzi, B., Muralidharan, K., *A Profile of the Indian Education System*, 2005.

Colby, S., Wicoff, K., *Aspire Public Schools: from 10 Schools to 6 Million Kids*, Bridgespan, 2006.

Coleman, J., *Equality of Educational Opportunity*, 1966.

Commission on No Child Left Behind, *Beyond NCLB*, 2007.

Cowen, N., *Swedish Lessons*, Civitas, 2008.

Cross City Campaign for Urban School Reform, *A Delicate Balance: District Policies and Classroom Practice*, 2005.

Csikszentmihalyi, M., *Flow: The Psychology of Optimal Experience*, Harper Perennial, 1990.

Csikszentmihalyi, M., *Good Business: Leadership, Flow and the Making of Meaning*, Penguin, 2003.

Cunha, F., Heckman, J., Lochner, L., Masterov, D., *Interpreting the Evidence on Life Cycle Skill Formation*, 2005

Currie, J., Thomas, D., *Early Test Scores, School Quality, and SES*, 1997.

Darling-Hammond, L., Bransford, J. (Eds.), *Preparing Teachers for a Changing World*, Jossey-Bass, 2005.

Day, C., *School Leadership for Systemic Improvement: Communities of Schools in Flanders, Belgium*, OECD, 2007.

Decker, P., Mayer, D., Glazerman, S., *The Effects of Teach For America: Findings From A National Evaluation*, 2004.

Dolton, P., Tremayne, A., Chung, T., *The Economic Cycle and Teacher Supply*, OECD, 2003.

Dunford, J., *Her Majesty's Inspectorate of Schools Since 1944*, Woburn, 1998.

Earl, L., Watson, N., Katz, S., *Large Scale Education Reform: Lifecycles and Implications for Sustainability*, CfBT, 2003.

Economist, "Bac to School," 6 September 2007.

Economist, "Gifted Children," 8 February 2007.

Economist, "Who Wants to be a Genius," 11 Jan 2001.

The Education Trust, *Gaining Traction, Gaining Ground*, 2005.

Education and Manpower Bureau (Hong Kong), *The Impact Study on the Effectiveness of External School Review in Enhancing School Improvement through School Self-Evaluation in Hong Kong*, 2006.

Education Policy Institute, *An Academic Impact Analysis of the Knowledge Is Power Program*, 2005.

Education Review Office, *The Quality of Year 2 Beginning Teachers*, 2004.

Ehrenberg, R., Brewer, D., Gamoran, A., Willms, D., "Does Class Size Matter," *Scientific American*, November 2001.

Elmore, R., *School Reform from the Inside Out*, Harvard Education Press, 2006.

Eurydice, *Education in Europe*, 2005.

Eurydice, *Evaluation of Schools Providing Compulsory Education in Europe*, 2004.

Filmer, D., Hasan, A., Pritchett, L., *A Millennium Learning Goal: Measuring Real Progress in Education*, 2006.

Fiske, E., Ladd, L., *When Schools Compete*, Brookings Institution, 2000.

Flora, C., "The Grandmaster Experiment," *Psychology Today*, July 2005.

Fordham, *The State of State Standards*, 2006.

Fuchs, T., Wößmann, L., *What Accounts for International Differences in Student Performance*, 2004.

Fullan, M., *Leading in a Culture of Change*, Jossey-Bass, 2007.

Fullan, M., "Leading Professional Learning" in *The School Administrator*, November 2006.

Fullan, M., *The Moral Imperative of School Leadership*, Corwin, 2003.

Fullan, M., *The New Meaning of Educational Change*, Teachers' College Press, 2007.

Fullan, M., *Professional Development is not Professional Learning*, 2007.

Fullan, M., *The Six Secrets of Change*, Jossey-Bass, 2008.

Fullan, M., Bertani, A., Quinn, J., "New Lessons For Districtwide Reform," in *Educational Leadership*, April 2004.

Fullan, M., Hill, P., Crévola, C., *Breakthrough*, Corwin Press, 2006.

Garet, M., Porter, A., Desimone, L., Binnan, B., Yoon, K., "What Makes Professional Development Effective? Results From a National Sample of Teachers," in *American Educational Research Journal*, 2001.

Garvin, D., "Building a Learning Organization" in Harvard Business School, *Harvard Business Review on Knowledge Management*, HBS Press, 1998.

Gasperini, L., *The Cuban Education System: Lessons and Dilemmas*, 1999.

Gladwell, M., "Most Likely to Succeed: How do we hire when we can't tell who's right for the job?" in *The New Yorker*, 15 December 2008.

Goh, C., Gopinathan, S., *The Development of Education in Singapore Since 1965*, 2006.

Goldhaber, D., Brewer, D., "Does Teacher Certification Matter? High School Teacher Certification Status and Student Achievement," *Educational Evaluation and Policy Analysis, Vol. 22, No. 2*, 2000.

Greene, J., *Education Myths*, Rowman & Littlefield, 2005.

Greene, J., Winters, M., Forster, G., *Testing High-Stakes Tests: Can We Believe the Results of Accountability Tests? (Civic Report No. 33)*, 2003.

Grubb, N., *Equity in Education Thematic Review: Finland*, 2005.

Gundlauch, E., Wößmann, L., "Better Schools for Europe," *EIB Papers*, 2001.

Hanushek, E., *Economic Outcomes and School Quality*, IAE, 2005.

Hanushek, E., "Some Findings from an Independent Investigation of the Tennessee STAR Experiment and from Other Investigations of Class Size Effects," *Educational Evaluation and Policy Analysis 21*, 1999.

Hanushek, E., Pace, R., *Who Chooses to Teach and Why*, 1995.

Hanushek, E., Raymond, M., *Does School Accountability Lead to Improved Student Performance*, 2004.

Hanushek, E., Rivkin, S., *How to Improve the Supply of High Quality Teachers*, 2003.

Hanushek, E., Wößmann, L., *Does Educational Tracking Affect Performance and Inequality? Differences-in-Differences Evidence across Countries*, 2005.

Hanushek, E., Wößmann, L., *The Role of Education Quality in Economic Growth*, World Bank, 2007.

Hart, B., Risley, T., "The 30 Million Word Gap by Age 3," *American Educator*, 2003.

Hartocollis, A., "Who Needs Education Schools," *New York Times*, 31 July 2005.

Haycock, K., *The Closing the Achievement Gap*, 2006.

Hays, C., "What Wal-Mart Knows About Customers' Habits," *New York Times*, 14 November 2004.

Headden, S., "Two Guys ... and a Dream," *US News*, 12 February 2006.

Hill, P., *School and Teacher Effectiveness in Victoria*, 1993.

HMI, *Ten Good Schools*, 1977.

Hopkins, D., *Every School a Great School*, McGraw Hill, 2007.

House of Commons, *Oral Evidence Taken Before the Children Schools and Families Committee*, 10 December 2007.

Hutchings, M., Maylor, U., Mendick, H., Menter, I., Smart, S., *An Evaluation of Innovative Approaches to Teacher Training on the Teach First Programme*, Institute for Policy Studies in Education, 2006.

IEA, *Progress in International Reading Literacy Study 2001*, 2002.

IEA, *Progress in International Reading Literacy Study 2006*, 2007.

IEA, *Trends in International Mathematics and Science Study 1995*, 1996.

IEA, *Trends in International Mathematics and Science Survey 2003*, 2004.

IEA, *Trends in International Mathematics and Science Survey 2007*, 2008.

Jordan, H., Mendro, R., Weerasinghe, D., *Teacher Effects on Longitudinal Student Achievement*, 1997.

Kane, T., Rockoff, J., Steiger, D., *What Does Certification Tell Us About Teacher Effectiveness?*, 2006.

Kennedy, A., Mullis, I., Martin, M., Throng, K., *PIRLS 2006 Encyclopaedia: A Guide to Reading Education in the Forty PIRLS 2006 Countries*, IEA, 2007.

Kim, E., and Han, Y., *Attracting, Developing, and Retaining Effective Teachers: Background Report for South Korea*, 2002.

Kopp, W., *One Day All Children*, Public Affairs, 2001.

Kotter, J., *Leading Change*, Harvard Business School Press, 1996.

Lareau, A., *Unequal Childhoods: Class, Race, and Family Life*, University of California Press, 2003.

Latin American Educational Quality Assessment Laboratory, *First International Comparative Study of Language, Mathematics, and Associated Factors in the Third and Fourth Grades*, UNESCO, 1998.

Lee, S., Goh, C., *Making Teacher Education Responsive and Relevant*, 2007.

Leithwood, K., Day, C., Sammons, P., Harris, A., Hopkins, D., *Seven Strong Claims About Successful School Leadership*, NCSL, 2006.

Leithwood, K., Day, C., Sammons, P., Harris, A., Hopkins, D., *Successful School Leadership: What it is and How it Influences Pupil Learning*, 2008.

Leschly, S., *New Leaders for New Schools*, HBS, 2002.

Leschly, S., *The Gates Foundation and Small High Schools*, 2003.

LeTendre, B., Roberts, B., *A National View of Certification of School Principals*, 2005.

Levin, B., Glaze, A., Fullan, M., "Results without Rancor or Ranking: Ontario's Success Story," in *Phi Delta Kappan*, December 2008.

Liker, J., *The Toyota Way*, McGraw Hill, 1994.

Linnakylä, P., Välijärvi, J., *Finnish Students' Performance in PISA*, 2003.

Lochner, L., Moretti, E., *The Effect of Education on Crime*, 2003.

Los Angeles Times, "Few Parents Move Their Children Out of Failing Schools," 8 November 2004.

Marzano, R., *A New Era of School Reform: Going Where the Research Takes Us*, 2000.

Matthews, J., "New Teacher Jolts KIPP," *Washington Post*, 19 December 2006.

Matthews, P., Sammons, P., *Improvement Through Inspection*, 2004.

McBeath, A., *Changing Rules and Roles: A Primer on School-based Decision Making*, Cross City Campaign for Urban School Reform, 2001.

McBeath, A., *Getting Districtwide Results*, 2006.

McBeath, A., *How Edmonton Does It and Why It Works*, 2003.

Michaelowa, K., Wechtler, A., *The Cost-Effectiveness of Inputs in Primary Education: Insights from the Literature and Recent Student Surveys for Sub-Saharan Africa*, 2006.

Milanowski, A., "An Exploration of the Pay Levels Needed to Attract Students with Mathematics, Science, and Technology Skills to a Career in K-12 Teaching," *Education Policy Analysis Archives*, 2003.

Ministry of Education (Finland), *Attracting, Developing, and Retaining Effective Teachers: Country Background Report for Finland*, 2003.

Ministry of Education (Finland), *Improving School Leadership*, 2007.

Ministry of Education (New Zealand), *Improving School Leadership*, 2007.

Mok, K., *Centralization and Decentralization: Educational Reforms and Changing Governance in Chinese Societies*, Kluwer, 2003.

Mok, K., Welch, A., *Globalization and Educational Restructuring in the Asia Pacific Region*, Palgrave, 2003.

Molin, J., *Improving School Leadership: National Background Report: Denmark*, 2007.

Moyer, D., "Training Daze," *Harvard Business Review*, October 2008.

NAEP, *A Closer Look At Charter Schools Using Hierarchical Linear Modelling*, 2006.

NAEP, *America's Charter Schools: Results from the NAEP 2003 Pilot Study*, 2004.

National Audit Office, *Improving Poorly Performing Schools in England*, 2006.

National Center for Education Statistics, *NAEP 2004: Trends in Academic Progress*, 2005.

National Center on Education and the Economy, *Tough Choices or Tough Times*, Jossey-Bass, 2007.

NCES, *Mapping 2005 State Proficiency Standards onto the NAEP Scales*, 2007.

NCSL, *Hard Federations of Small Primary Schools*, 2008.

NCTQ, *Increasing the Odds*, 2004.

NCTQ, *What Education Schools Aren't Teaching*, 2006.

Ndaruhutse, S., *Grade Repetition in Primary Schools in Sub-Saharan Africa*, CfBT, 2008.

Norwegian Directorate for Education and Training, *Improving School Leadership: Country Background Report for Norway*, 2007.

OECD, *Attracting, Developing, and Retaining Effective Teachers*, 2005.

OECD, *Completing the Foundation for Lifelong Learning*, 2004.

OECD, *The Definition and Selection of Key Competencies*, 2005.

OECD, *Education at a Glance*, 2000-2008.

OECD, *Improving School Leadership*, 2008.

OECD, *Literacy in the Information Age*, 2000.

OECD, *Networks of Innovation*, 2003.

OECD, *New School Management Approaches*, 2001.

OECD, *Personalizing Education*, 2006.

OECD, *PISA 2000*, 2001.

OECD, *PISA 2003*, 2004.

OECD, *PISA 2006*, 2007.

OECD, *Reviews of National Policies on Education: Estonia*, 2001.

OECD, *Starting Strong II: Early Childhood Education and Care*, 2006.

OECD, *What Makes School Systems Perform*, 2004.

Ofsted, *Mathematics: Understanding the Score*, 2008.

Ofsted, *Rising to the Challenge: A Review of the Teach First Initial Teacher Training Program*, 2008.

Olson, L., "State Test Programs Mushroom as NCLB Mandate Kicks In," *Education Week*, 30 November 2006.

Parks, G., *The High Scope Perry Preschool Project*, 2000.

Patrinos, H., *School Choice in Denmark*, 2001.

Perris, L., *Implementing Education Reforms in New Zealand: 1987-1997*, 1998.

Peters, T., Waterman, R., *In Search of Excellence*, Profile, 2003.

Peterson, K., Abbott, M., *The Power of Early Success 1998-2004*, 2005.

Podgursky, M., Springer, M., *Teacher Performance Pay: A Review*, 2006.

Price Waterhouse Coopers, *An Independent Study into School Leadership*, 2007.

Pritchett, L., *Towards a New Consensus for Addressing the Global Challenge of the Lack of Education*, 2004.

Ramsey, G., *Quality Matters*, 2000.

Rand, *Partners in Pittsburg Public Schools' Excellence for All Initiative*, 2007

Raymond, M., Hanushek, E., "High Stakes Research" in *Education Next*, 2003.

Rivkin, S., Hanushek, E., Kain, J., "Teachers, Schools, and Academic Achievement," in *Economentrica*, March 2005.

Rosenthal, M., et al., *Early Experience with Pay-For-Performance from Concept to Practice*, April 2005

Rothman, S., *Achievement in Literacy and Numeracy by Australian 14-year olds 1975-1998*, ACER, 2002.

Rothstein, R., *The Myths and Realities of America's Student Achievement*, Century Foundation, 1998.

Rowe, K., "The Importance of Teacher Quality," *Issue Analysis No. 22*, 2002.

Sander, W., Rivers, J., *Cumulative and Residual Effects of Teachers on Future Student Academic Achievement*, 1996.

Johnes, G., Johnes, J. (Eds.), *International Handbook on the Economics of Education*, Edward Elgar, 2004.

Schleicher, A., *Learning For Tomorrow's World: Results From PISA 2003*, 2005.

Schleicher, A., *Why Education is Key for Europe's Success,* Lisbon Council, 2006.

Schütz, G., West, M., Wößmann, L., *School Accountability, Autonomy, Choice, and the Equity of Student Achievement: International Evidence from PISA 2003*, OECD, 2007.

Schwartzman, S., *The Challenges of Education in Brazil*, 2003.

Schweinhart, L., *The High Scope Perry Preschool Study Through Age 40,* 2005.

Schwille, J., Dembélé, M., *Global Perspectives on Teacher Learning: Improving Policy and Practice*, UNESCO, 2007.

Sclafani, S., *Rethinking Human Capital in Education: Singapore as a Model for Teacher Development*, Aspen Institute, 2008.

Seong, D., *Strategic Management of Educational Development in Singapore*, 2006.

Shapson, S., Wright, E., Eason, G., Fitzgerald, J., "An Experimental Study on the Effects of Class Size," *American Educational Research Journal*, 1980.

Shvidler, E., "All the Right Moves," *Haaretz*.

Smith, A., Faux, T., *Education, Conflict, and International Development*, DfID, 2003.

Stannard, J., Huxford, L., *The Literacy Game: The Story of the National Literacy Strategy*, Routledge, 2007.

Statistics Commission, *Measuring Standards in English Primary Schools*, February 2005.

Stossel, J., "How Lack of Choice Cheats Our Kids Out of a Good Education," *ABC News*, 13 January 2006.

Swanson, C., *Who Graduates?*, Urban Institute, 2003.

Swift, F., *Education in Ancient Israel*, Open Court, 1919.

Sylva, K., Melhuish, E., Sammons, P., Siraj-Blatchford, I., Taggart, B., Eliot, K., *The Effective Provision of Pre-School Education Project: Findings from the Pre-school Period*, 2003.

Talyor, B., "Urban Superintendents Hard to Keep," *USA Today*, 30 September 2008.

Taylor, N., "What's Wrong with South African Schools," *JET Education Conference*, 2008.

Taylor, N., Prinsloo, C., *The Quality Learning Project*, 2005.

TDA, *Performance Profiles Aggregate Dataset*, 2007.

Teach First, *Lessons from the Front: 1,000 New Teachers Speak Up*, 2007.

Tee, N., "The Singapore School and the School Excellence Model," *Educational Research for Policy and Practice 2*, 2003.

Telegraph, "Queen Takes All," 16 January 2002.

Times, *Top 100 Graduate Employers*, 2007.

UNESCO, *Children Out of School: Measuring Exclusion from Primary Education*, 2005.

UNESCO, *Education for All Global Monitoring Report*, 2005-2008.

Välijärvi, J., Linnakylä, P., Kupari, P., Reinikainen, P., Arffman, I., *The Finnish Success in PISA - And Some Reasons for It*, OECD, 2003.

Värri, K., Alava, J., *School Management Training (Finland)*, 2005.

Vygotsky, L., *Mind in Society* edited by Cole, M., (et al.), Harvard, 1978.

Walsh, K., *If Wishes Were Horses: The Reality Behind Teacher Quality Findings*, 2007.

Wasley, P., Lear, R., "Small Schools, Real Gains," *Educational Leadership*, 2001.

Waters, J., Marzano, R., McNulty, B., *Balanced Leadership*, 2006.

Winkler, D., *The Efficiency of Public Education in Uganda*, World Bank, 2007.

World Bank, "Getting Teachers and Doctors to Report to Work," 23 March 2006.

Wößmann, L., Schütz, G., *Efficiency and Equity in European Education and Training Systems*, 2006.

Wylie, C., Mitchell, L., *Sustaining Development in a Decentralized System: Lessons from New Zealand*, 2003.

Index